Step It Up

A Multilevel Reading-Writing Text for Learners of English

M. E. Sokolik
University of California
Berkeley

Ann Arbor
THE UNIVERSITY OF MICHIGAN PRESS

ISBN 0-472-03056-6
Published in the United States of America by
The University of Michigan Press
Manufactured in the United States of America

2008 2007 2006 2005 4 3 2 1

Acknowledgments

Grateful acknowledgment is made to the following authors, publishers, and journals for permission to reprint previously published materials.

The Associated Press for obituaries of Frida Kahlo and Diego Rivera from the *New York Times,* © 1954. Reprinted with permission of The Associated Press.

Ray Bradbury for publicity photo of himself. Photo by Tom Victor. Reprinted by permission.

Business 2.0 for "Ask Evelyn: Closing the Cultural Gap," November 2003 issue. Copyright © 2003 Time Inc. All rights reserved.

Canada's Digital Collections for "Trip Inland in Summer," *http://www.collections.gc.ca/.*

Don Congdon Associates, Inc. for "I See You Never" by Ray Bradbury from *The New Yorker.* Reprinted by permission of Don Congdon Associates, Inc. Copyright © 1947, renewed 1974 by Ray Bradbury.

Corbis for photos of Overworked Secretary Working at Messy Desk, Schoolgirl Reading Book, Fruit and Vegetable Background, and Skyscrapers and Mount Fuji.

Daily Princetonian Publishing Company, Inc. for photo of John Nash. Reprinted by permission.

Dorset Fine Arts for image of "Summer Travelers" by Jamasie Teevee, *http://www.collections.gc.ca/.*

Farrar, Straus and Giroux, LLC, for excerpts from *Slaves in the Family* by Edward Ball. Copyright © 1998 by Edward Ball. Reprinted by permission of Farrar, Straus and Giroux, LLC.

Robert Fox for "A Fable." Reprinted by permission of Robert Fox.

Francis Goldin Agency, Inc. for "Going to Japan" from *Small Wonder: Essays* by Barbara Kingsolver. Copyright © 2002 by Barbara Kingsolver.

HarperCollins Publishers for "Going to Japan" [pp. 176-9] from *Small Wonder: Essays* by Barbara Kingsolver. Copyright © 2002 by Barbara Kingsolver. Reprinted by permission of HarperCollins Publishers Inc.; for submitted excerpt totaling 469 words from *Krakatoa: The Day the World Exploded* by Simon Winchester. Copyright © 2003 by Simon Winchester. Reprinted by permission of HarperCollins Publishers, Inc.

John Hawkins & Associates, Inc. for excerpt from *The Autobiography of Malcolm X* by Malcolm X and Alex Haley, copyright © 1964 by Alex Haley and Malcolm X. Copyright © 1965 by Alex Haley and Betty Shabazz.

Houghton Mifflin for an excerpt from *Silent Spring* by Rachel Carson. Copyright © 1962 by Rachel Carson, renewed 1990 by Roger Christie; for excerpt from *How to Read a French Fry* by Russ Parsons. Copyright © 2001 by Russ Parsons. Reprinted by permission of Houghton Mifflin Company. All rights reserved.

Deborah Kopka for illustrations.

Library of Congress, Prints and Photographs Division, for photographs of: Albert Einstein, LC-USZ62-106041; Helen Keller and Anne Sullivan, LC-USZ62-78999; Malcolm X, LC-USZ62-112131; Frida Kahlo, LC-USZ62-117438; Diego Rivera, LC-USZ62-88104; Stowage of British slave ship Brookes, LC-USZ62-44000; The island and volcano of Krakatoa, LC-USZ62-8590; Jacques Cousteau, LC-USZ62-119519; and Rachel Carson, LC-USZ62-111207.

The Minnesota Historical Society for "Ojibway Grand Medicine Ceremony" by Monroe P. Killy, Photograph Collection, 1932.

Mystic Seaport for "AMISTAD Under Sail," No. 2000-6-491, © Mystic Seaport, Mystic, CT. Reprinted by permission.

National Geographic Society News Feature by Hillary Mayell. Copyright 2002 by National Geographic Society. Reproduced with permission of National Geographic Society Textbook via Copyright Clearance Center.

Penguin Group (USA) Inc. for material from *The Log from the Sea of Cortez* by John Steinbeck, copyright 1941 by John Steinbeck and Edward F. Ricketts. Copyright renewed © 1969 by John Steinbeck and Edward F. Ricketts, Jr. Used by permission of Viking Penguin, a division of Penguin Group (USA) Inc.

The Port Huron Times Herald for "The Road Back" by Deanna Weinger, July 1, 2003.

Random House for excerpt from *The Autobiography of Malcolm X* by Malcolm X and Alex Haley, copyright © 1964 by Alex Haley and Malcolm X. Copyright © 1965 by Alex Haley and Betty Shabazz. Used by permission of Random House, Inc.

Sarah Reaume for illustrations.

San Francisco Chronicle for "Japanese Scientists Predicted Big Quake" by Keay Davidson. Reproduced with permission of *San Francisco Chronicle* in the format Textbook via Copyright Clearance Center.

Aram and Lucy Saroyan for "The Summer of the Beautiful White Horse" by William Saroyan.

Scientific American for an adapted version of "Birth of the Modern Diet" by Rachel Laudan, August 2000. Copyright © 2000 by Scientific American, Inc. All rights reserved.

Sterling Lord Literistic Inc., for excerpt from *Krakatoa: The Day the World Exploded* by Simon Winchester. Copyright © 2003 by Simon Winchester.

Thomson Learning for "Reading as a Reader" from Read to Write, 3rd edition by Donald M. Murray, © 1993. Reprinted with permission of Heinle, a division of Thomson Learning: *www.thomsonrights.com.* Fax: 800 730-2216.

Every effort has been made to contact the copyright holders for permission to reprint borrowed material. We regret any oversights that may have occurred and will rectify them in future printings of this book.

Contents

To the Instructor

Mixed-level classes are a challenge for even the most experienced instructor. They present not only a mixture of levels, but a mixture of goals that often seem to work against each other. For example, you may recognize that each level of students needs a different approach or different materials, and yet you want to create a classroom atmosphere that is inclusive for all students, regardless of proficiency level. You may want to develop the best materials for each student's needs and progress, yet your time or curriculum limits what you can do for students at different levels, leaving you feeling pulled in different directions.

This book was written with these competing goals in mind. In addition, it focuses on turning the conflict between goals into potentially powerful learning opportunities. Mixed-level classes, for example, provide a wonderful opportunity for students to challenge themselves, to learn to communicate with a wide variety of speakers, and to fill in the gaps in their learning, no matter what their level. By focusing on language at their own levels and then broadening the discussion to include a larger group, students develop confidence in their abilities.

I also hope that through using this text, instructors and students alike will reconsider the idea of "level" to some extent. Students often have strengths and weaknesses with different skills or even different topics. Their former education or job skills may have given them a background that makes them "advanced" in some areas and "beginning" in others. *Step It Up* can also address the needs of learners who do not fall into neat categories and may find doing work at different levels helps them to fill in the gaps of their knowledge of English.

The Structure of This Book

This textbook is divided into 10 chapters, each focusing on a different academic discipline. There are also suggestions for additional reading and activities in the appendices at the back. Each chapter begins with an **Icebreaker** activity. This activity serves two purposes: it gives students a general sense of the chapter's theme, as well as an opportunity to take part in a pre-reading discussion. The instructor may choose to pair or group students across ability levels or within ability levels for this activity. The Icebreaker is intended as a warm-up activity, encouraging students from the start to be comfortable with each other regardless of their level.

Next is the **Chapter Preview.** This activity serves to activate any prior knowledge a student may have about the subject matter of the chapter. It asks simple yes-no questions for each step that students can answer on their own. It also asks them to expand upon their answer with a short written response.

Each chapter then has three inter-related readings at three levels—called the **First Step, Second Step,** and **Third Step.** An icon identifies the levels of readings and activities:

First Step Second Step Third Step

This textbook focuses strongly on vocabulary development as it relates to reading and writing. Each reading passage is preceded by a vocabulary exercise focusing on challenging, but common academic words found in the reading assignment. (The vocabulary words are shaded in the readings.) The vocabulary exercise types vary—at the first and second steps, they may be dictionary look-up activities, matching exercises, or fill-in the blanks. At the third step, sentence creation activities are the most common. The difficulty level of the vocabulary and the exercise type increases with the increasing steps. The purpose of the introductory vocabulary tasks is to highlight and become familiar with key vocabulary that will be found in the reading. When students begin the reading, they will find the same vocabulary items have been highlighted within the text. This is done to draw attention to the words that have been introduced.

The readings represent different genres within the disciplines: short stories, newspaper articles, expository essays, biographies, letters to the editor, how-to articles, and so forth. Many of the readings have been chosen to expose students to well-known writers, both past and present. The writing of Helen Keller, John Steinbeck, William Saroyan, and Rachel Carson, as well as many others, will become familiar to students as they work through the text. Additionally, reading notes are added occasionally to the readings to explain cultural or historical facts that may not be familiar.

The readings are followed immediately by comprehension questions (**Check Your Understanding**) of different types. Again, simpler true/false or matching exercises are found at the lower steps, while more open-ended questions are found at the advanced steps. The comprehension questions focus on recall of facts and ideas from the reading passages, and some level of drawing inferences at the higher steps. The comprehension questions can be done alone or in pairs or small groups.

After the comprehension questions are group discussion questions. These are intended to be done in groups who have worked on the same readings. These questions are related to the reading, but they invite the students to relate the readings to their own experiences and to talk about things that are familiar. One suggestion for successful group discussion is to assign roles within the group. Ask one student to take notes on the group's responses, another to lead the group in asking questions and encouraging participation, another student to watch the time, and so forth. Group participation will increase significantly if students know what role they are expected to play.

Finally, there is more focused work on specific language areas appropriate to the readings and their levels. These areas arise out of the readings themselves—that is, the language focus activity comes out of a prevalent linguistic feature of each reading. These activities may deal with prepositions or word endings at the lower steps, and more complex ideas such as metaphors or complex syntax at the Third Step.

The **Chapter Wrap-Up** activities include speaking and writing tasks, some which are presented specifically by level, and some of which are appropriate for all levels. These are an important feature of each chapter. These activities allow the students to bring the expertise they have gained from their reading, whether it is at Step One or Step Three, to the rest of the group. Since all students are reading in the same academic discipline, there will be some familiarity with the topics discussed, and a heightened level of understanding and interest at all levels as a result. A fourth icon——identifies the items that are intended for mixed-level groups.

The chapters are arranged generally starting with the humanities and social science fields, moving into the sciences. However, they can be assigned in any order. It is recommended, however, that Chapter 1 be done first, since it covers basic study skills and reading strategies. The information in this chapter will help the students as they work through the book.

Students may be assigned to levels according to any system established by you or your institution, or they may choose the level that they believe suits them, according to their own assessment of their skills or the material presented in the chapter. For argument's sake, the first step can be considered *intermediate;* the second step, *high-intermediate/low-advanced;* and the third step, *advanced.* Assume a post-secondary audience.

Similarly, this textbook may be used over the course of two or three terms with the same group of students. Students can progress through the steps presented in the book until they have completed all the material—moving from the simpler material to the more complex, while working on a large variety of readings and activities.

This textbook was written in the hopes that instructors in multilevel classes will find ways to keep all students involved not only with the course curriculum, but also with each other. Each voice, whether beginning, intermediate, or advanced, has something to contribute in the classroom.

To the Student

This book may look different from other books you have used. It has readings and activities for different levels of students. You will see different symbols to tell you the level, or "step," of a reading or activity:

First Step   Second Step   Third Step

Another symbol— —tells you that an activity is for everyone.

Your instructor will tell you which level you should work on. However, if you are at the First Step or Second Step, try some of the materials at a higher step. This will help you to learn even more. If you are already at the Third Step, look at material in the lower steps. They may contain ideas or words you haven't seen before. This also will help you to review your learning, which is an important part of being a good language learner.

A class with different levels of students can be a challenge for everyone. If you are at the First Step, it may seem difficult to speak in front of others, especially if you think their English is better than yours is. However, you will learn faster if you do.

If you are at the Second or Third Step, you may worry that you aren't making progress fast enough. However, learning to communicate with a variety of speakers will help you to become a more effective English speaker and learner, too.

The world is full of English speakers with different accents and different language abilities. Your class is a good opportunity to learn to communicate in the "real world."

CHAPTER

1 An Introduction

Study Skills

Icebreaker

An *icebreaker* is something that "breaks the ice" or starts a conversation. Ask a partner these questions. Write down the answers so you remember them.

1. What is your name?
2. Do you enjoy reading and writing? Why?
3. Do you have a favorite book or writer (in any language)? Describe the book or writer.

Now, introduce your partner to your class. Tell your classmates what you learned about him or her.

CHAPTER PREVIEW

Do you have good study skills? Answer these questions to find out:

1. Is your study space organized? *yes* *no*
2. Do you take good notes on your reading or lectures? *yes* *no*
3. Have you tried different reading skills and strategies? *yes* *no*

Explain your answer: ______________________________

____

____

____

This chapter will give you a lot of information on study skills: organizing your space, taking good notes, and reading strategies.

First Step

Vocabulary

These words are in the reading. Do you know what they mean?

1. *convenient*
   a. useful
   b. easy
   c. put away
2. *organize*
   a. make
   b. arrange
   c. keep
3. *planner*
   a. dictionary
   b. help
   c. date book
4. *respect*
   a. be thoughtful
   b. help
   c. keep
5. *refresh*
   a. to be tired
   b. to remember something
   c. to get more energy

Reading

Five Ideas to Help You Study

1. Choose a good study area. Choose a place where your study materials are convenient, and where you can get right to work. Organize your space so you can find important materials.
2. Quiet or noisy? Do you need quiet when you study, or do you like music or television noise? Will your study space be near any of these things?
   - ☐ a place where people are talking
   - ☐ a television
   - ☐ a telephone

   Find a study place that fits your need for noise or quiet.
3. Schedule your study time. Mark on your calendar or planner the times you will eat, sleep, exercise, go to class, work, and study. Keep to your schedule. Do not mix personal activities with your study time. Make a schedule for studying and for personal activities.
4. Get help from others. If you live with others, ask them to respect your study time. Ask them not to interrupt you. If you want quiet, ask them to keep the television or music low.
5. Take breaks. Do not spend your free time at your desk. Go for a walk. Read a book. Talk to a friend. When you take a break, you help refresh your mind.

Check Your Understanding

Choose the correct answer.

1. If you organize your study space
   a. it will be quiet.
   b. you will find important materials.
   c. it won't be near the phone or television.
2. What should you write on your planner?
   a. just your study times
   b. your class schedule
   c. all of your activities
3. Which statement is true?
   a. A break will help refresh your mind.
   b. When you study, you must stay at your desk all the time.
   c. You should mix personal activities and study activities.

Group Discussion

Talk about these questions with your group or a partner.

1. Do you listen to music when you study? If so, what kind of music do you like?
2. Where is your favorite place to study?
3. How many hours do you study each week?

Language Focus: Idioms

These idioms, or special expressions, are found in your reading. The vocabulary may look simple, but the meaning may not be clear. Talk about the meaning of these idioms with a classmate or your teacher. Write the meanings in the spaces.

take a break ______________________________

____

keep the music low ______________________________

____

keep to a schedule ______________________________

____

get right to work ______________________________

____

Read the descriptions. Then fill in the idiom that fits the description.

Example: Marta studied for three hours. Right now, she is watching television. Marta is taking a break.

1. Larry's mother is sleeping. He needs to ________________, so he doesn't wake her up.
2. Minh has a test tomorrow. It's already 7:00. She needs to ________________ so she can finish her reading.
3. Ivan has to work, go to school, and take care of his family. He writes everything in his planner so he can ________________.
4. Lena and Roger have been studying for five hours. They should ________________ so they don't get too tired.
5. Mr. Young wants to go home and ________________ so he can finish studying tonight.

Now, choose one of the idioms from the list and write a sentence about yourself using that idiom.

6. ______________________________

____

Second Step

Vocabulary

These words are in the reading. Do you know what they mean? Discuss the meaning of these words with a classmate or your teacher. Write the meanings in the spaces.

1. *technique:* ______________________________

   ____

2. *omit:* ______________________________

   ____

3. *keyword:* ______________________________

   ____

4. *clarify:* ______________________________

   ____

5. *reinforce:* ______________________________

   ____

6. *assimilate:* ______________________________

   ____

Reading

Reading Note: *Cornell University is located in Ithaca, New York. It was founded by Ezra Cornell in 1868.*

The Cornell Note-Taking System

Cornell University Professor Walter Pauk developed the Cornell note-taking system to help his students organize their notes. Today, Pauk's note-taking technique is a popular system all over the world.

Here's how it works: First, divide your paper into two columns: approximately 2.5 inches (6.25 centimeters) on the left, and 6 inches (15.25 centimeters) on the right. Then follow these six steps.

Record. In the column on the right side of the paper, **record,** or write down, as many facts and ideas as you can. If you are in a lecture, don't try to write every word that the lecturer says. Also, your notes do not have to be spelled correctly or be grammatical. Omit *a* and *the* or other words that aren't necessary for understanding. Learn to write brief sentences, and use keywords to help you remember main points. Use abbreviations when you can.

Reduce or question. After the lecture, read through your notes. The next step is to **reduce** important facts and ideas to keywords or phrases, and to write questions about those facts and ideas. Write keywords, phrases, and questions in the smaller column on the left. These words and phrases are memory aids; when you review them, you will recall the ideas or facts. The questions help to clarify the meanings of the facts and ideas.

Recite. To recite is to say *aloud* and *in your own words* the facts and ideas you are trying to learn. It is a good way to learn because hearing your thoughts helps you to improve your thought process. Stating ideas and facts in your own words helps you to think about the meaning of the information.

To recite, cover your notes in the large column, and leave the keywords and questions uncovered. Read each keyword or question, then recite, aloud and in your own words, the information. If your answer is correct, continue through your lecture notes by reciting aloud.

Reflect. Reflection means thinking about the information you have learned. This goes beyond learning what is in your notes—it reinforces deeper learning by relating facts and ideas to other knowledge. For example, you might **reflect** by asking yourself: *How do these facts and ideas apply to what I already know? Why is knowing these ideas important?*

Review. When you **review** your notes, you remember the ideas better. Try to review your notes every night or a few times a week by *reciting,* not just rereading. If you plan brief review sessions every week, you will learn and remember more than if you cram the night before a test. You will feel less stressed, too.

Recapitulate. To **recapitulate** means to summarize. You should summarize your notes at the bottom of the note page in the smaller column. Take a few minutes after you have reduced, recited, and reflected to recapitulate the facts and ideas in your notes. This will help you assimilate information from the lecture. A summary is not a word-for-word rewriting of your notes. Write it in your own words, and include the main points you want to remember from your notes. Reading through your summaries in preparation for a test is a good review technique. There are three ways to summarize:

1. Summarize each page of notes at the bottom of each page.
2. Summarize the entire lecture on the last page.
3. Combine techniques 1 and 2.

EXAMPLE: Cornell Note-Taking Format

Subject: Notetaking Date: 4/2/2005

Main Ideas	Details
Cornell notes	• Walter Pauk created. • Use for outline of course, chap., or lecture. • Organized by main ideas & details. • Can be as detailed as needed. • Take notes as given by instructor or text in orderly fashion. • After class, write summary to clarify & reinforce learning & assist memory. • Can be used as study tool 1. Define terms or explain ideas listed on left side. 2. Identify ideas or keyword based on definition on right side.
Summary: There are different ways that you can take notes. The Cornell method works well when the information is given in an organized way and allows for more detail.	

Check Your Understanding

Mark *true* or *false* for each question.

1. It is important that your notes be correctly spelled and grammatical.

   true *false*

2. Using keywords will help you to remember your main ideas.

   true *false*

3. Writing questions in your notes will help you explain the ideas you heard.

   true *false*

4. When you recite from your notes, you should cover the small column and leave the large column uncovered.

   true *false*

5. You can strengthen your understanding through the process of *reflection.*

   true *false*

6. One way to recapitulate your notes is to rewrite them word-for-word.

   true *false*

7. You should summarize your notes only on the last page.

   true *false*

Group Discussion

Talk about these questions with your group or a partner.

1. Do you think you are a good note-taker? Explain your answer.
2. Have you tried the Cornell system yet? If so, describe your experience using it.
3. Why is it important to take notes?

Language Focus: Preposition Practice

This reading gives a lot of "how-to" instructions and uses a lot of prepositions. See how many you can use correctly. Choose from the list. You will use some words more than once. Some blanks do not require prepositions.

Example: You can also summarize everything ___on___ the last page.

into *on* *in* *of* *to* *at* *from* *by* *for*

1. Divide your paper ________ two columns: 2.5 inches ________ the left and 6 inches ________ the right.
2. Record your ideas ________ the column ________ the right side ________ the paper.
3. Reduce facts ________ keywords or phrases.
4. Put your ideas ________ your own words.
5. Ask ________ yourself: How do these facts apply ________ what I already know?
6. Summarize your notes ________ the bottom ________ the note page.
7. You will assimilate ________ information ________ the lecture.
8. Organize your notes ________ main ideas and details.
9. Identify your ideas based ________ the definitions ________ the right side ________ the paper.
10. The Cornell method allows ________ the addition ________ details.
11. Now, write instructions for where to draw the heart in the box. Use prepositions in your instructions.

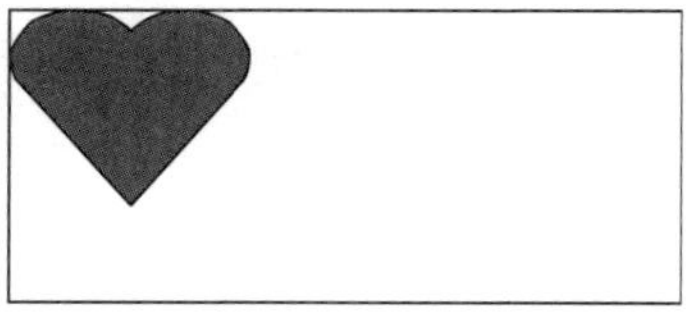

____

____

Third Step

Vocabulary

These words and phrases are in the reading. Find them in an English-English dictionary. Discuss their definition with a classmate or your teacher. Write the meanings, and in your own words, write a sample sentence that shows you understand the meaning.

Example: biochemistry: The study of the chemical substances and processes in living things; "biological chemistry."

Sample sentence: Biochemistry is a required course for students who want to be doctors.

1. *standings:* ______________________________

   ____

   Sample sentence: ______________________________

   ____

2. *swooping:* ______________________________

   ____

   Sample sentence: ______________________________

   ____

3. *inevitable:* ______________________________

   ____

   Sample sentence: ______________________________

   ____

4. *monograph:* ______________________________

____

Sample sentence: ______________________________

____

5. *pun:* ______________________________

____

Sample sentence: ______________________________

____

6. *cannibalism:* ______________________________

____

Sample sentence: ______________________________

____

7. *bog down in:* ______________________________

____

Sample sentence: ______________________________

____

8. *concise:* ______________________________

____

Sample sentence: ______________________________

____

9. *compression:* ______________________________

____

Sample sentence: ______________________________

____

Reading

Reading Note: *Try to practice the techniques described in the following essay as you read it.*

Reading as a Reader

excerpt from *Read to Write*
by Donald M. Murray

About the Author: Donald M. Murray is a Pulitzer Prize–winning journalist. He is Professor Emeritus of English at the University of New Hampshire. His books on writing include Write to Learn, The Craft of Revision, *and many others.*

The student in any field—medicine, public safety, language study, computer technology, environmental studies, sociology, biochemistry, political science, engineering, history, hotel management, law, business—finds it is essential to be an effective reader. Reading is increasingly important in a complex, global, technical society. We depend on the communication of an enormous amount of information and in such a world, information, even more than money, means power. We may read books, memos, newspapers, or we may read a computer screen or printout, but read we must if we are to understand and participate in our world, to know and to influence what is going on. We also read to write, to learn the craft that not only allows us to receive information but also to discover what we know and share it.

Reading for Information

When we read for information we experience the text in a different way. Depending on the information we seek, we may not want to enter into the story, and we do not much care how the writing is written, as long as the writing does not get in the way of the information we need. Our newspapers know we want information on stocks and football standings, and so they give us this information in the form of tables and listings. That writing is hardly "written" at all. Other times we need information that is hidden in a normal text of sentences and paragraphs. In that case we have to mine the text and extract the information we need. In this kind of reading we may choose to stand apart from the text, not to be involved in but simply to make use of what is said.

Scanning

To extract information from a text we need to scan, swooping over the text, looking for any clues that may help us find where the information is. We may turn first to an index or table of contents to see if it will tell us where the information we need is placed. In the case of an academic article we may read the abstract, a summary paragraph usually printed in small type at the beginning of the article to serve information gatherers and save them time.

Watching for Road Signs

If we think the text has the information we need, we should run through it, paying attention to chapter headings, cross-heads (such as the one above, "Watching for Road Signs"), illustrations, diagrams, or other signals designed to help us get to the information we need. When we confront the text itself we should look for key words that will tell us that the information may be nearby. For example, if we are looking for information on the low salaries of women office workers, we may look for such words as "secretaries," "file clerks," "typists," "receptionists," "salaries," "wages," "compensation," "sexism," "prejudice," "women," "girls," "office workers," and so on. We can run through many pages of type easily, stopping only when we see something that tells us the information may be nearby.

Making Notes

In reading for information we usually have a notebook or note cards handy so that we can put down the information we find. If the information is to be quoted directly, we should put quotation marks around it so that we know when we come to use it that the note is precisely as the author presented it. If we are to put the information in our own words it's helpful to do that immediately. It's also important to note the context in which the information was presented. The context for the information on office workers might be a feminist political statement, a report by a male scholar, a study by a union that wants to organize office workers, a statement by a corporation, or a survey by a government agency. It is most important that the note include the precise reference so that it can be included in the text and so that you and your reader can go back and find the information. This means the title of the publication, the author, and all of the details about the publication itself.

Reading for Understanding

Our most important reading occurs when we read to comprehend everything that a text has to teach us. We read for the experience of the text and we read for the information we can mine from it—and more. Reading stocks our mind with information and connections between pieces of information—theories, ideas, concepts, principles—that grow and change as we grow and change, experiencing, integrating all that we take in from living and thinking. We read to learn, to stimulate our minds, and so we have to learn to read well enough to make intellectual use of a great variety of texts, including many which are not easy to read. Some of them are difficult because the subject matter is difficult and the author has not been able to—or is writing for a specialized audience and feels no need to—simplify it for a general reader. Other books are difficult because the author does not write well but still has brought together information and ideas that are significant. All our lives we will be reading texts that are difficult for us to read. We will learn about a subject, read intensely in that area, get to know significant but difficult authors, and find it relatively easy to read what was once difficult; but, at the same time, we will continue to be learners, reading in new areas, and meeting new and challenging authors.

This process of lifelong education has become true for many people who have not considered themselves intellectuals or who did not imagine they would continue to learn—or have to continue to learn—after graduation. We live, however, in a society in which change seems to be the only constant. People advised me, for example, not to leave jobs with companies that no longer exist. Some security. The best security is an education that teaches you how to learn so you can adapt to the inevitable changes life will bring. Guess who laughed at writing on a word processor and found himself using one a few weeks later?

We all have difficult friends who are worth the effort, and you will have difficult authors to read whose articles, stories, poems, manuals, monographs, plays, and books—fiction and nonfiction—are worth the effort. We have to learn strategies for dealing with these texts. We do not need to use these strategies all the time, but we do need to have them on hand when we cannot understand what we are reading and so cannot even tell if the text is worth reading.

Who Are You?

The first step toward understanding is to know what you bring to the text as a reader. If a police officer, black or white, is assigned to a neighborhood, he or she must first know what prejudices, what stereotypes, what beliefs, what fears he or she wears with the badge. Each of us looks at the same neighborhood with significant differences, depending on our experience and our background. The same thing is true of a reader.

Expert readers know what they don't know and what they know as they approach a text. They know that their prejudices, preconceptions, personal background, and experiences affect the way they read the text. We all come to a book with a complicated inventory of information, ideas, and opinions that combine to make the text our own. We have begun to realize it is important to understand this. Every text is different for every reader. That doesn't mean we can't agree on what the text says, because we can, in discussion, usually work out a common understanding. It does mean that we often get to that understanding in very different ways. And it certainly can include the fact that we may disagree about what the text says. The text is not separate from the reader. As the reader reads the text becomes what is read. If you see, for example, a group of teenagers with different colored skins fighting, what each observer sees is powerfully colored, pun intended, by the observer's own background. Often there is not just one truth, but many truths. And we see through our own eyes, our own experiences, our own knowledge.

Who's the Author?

Once you know who you are—at least who you are in relation to this subject—then it may help to know who the writer is. Usually there are short biographies or an identifying sentence that tells who the writer is and what the writer's authority is to write this piece: "Norbert Morrison, now a Congressman from Iowa, has been practicing cannibalism since his Freshman year in college." If you think that the background of the author is vital to your understanding of the piece, then you can use the standard reference books, such as *Who's Who* and *Current Biography*, in the library to discover what you need to know about the writer.

What's the Form?

It may help to understand the piece we are reading if we know the genre or form in which it is written. This sounds obvious, but notice how many people use the term "novel," which means a fictional story, a work of the imagination, to describe nonfiction books of history or biography which are supposed to be based on documentable facts. It may help you understand the piece you are reading if you know it is a profile, a short biography written by someone other than the subject, or an autobiographical essay in which the person is writing about himself or herself. Part of form is purpose. In an argument the author wants to persuade us, but in a personal essay about the same subject the author may simply want to entertain. In a news story about the same subject, the writer may simply want to deliver objective fact.

What's the Context?

It helps to know the context or the nature of the world in which the piece was written. Pieces that were written during the Vietnam War, when there was both strong opposition to the war and powerful support for the war, may be confusing to a young reader who did not experience the pressure from both sides.

The reader should know the point of view of the publication in which an article is published. Some political magazines, for example, have a conservative point of view. Others are liberal. The reader needs to know that context. It may help, for example, to know that the discussion of a nuclear plant is written in a context of concern for human safety, for the environment, or for the economy.

Reading the Front Matter

Clues to questions of the writer's authority and the context of the book or article may be found by reading the notes about authors in a magazine or the material published on the dust jacket of a book or on a title page. It is often a good idea, for example, to see where the book was published. It may be significant to know that a book about Vietnam was published first in France, a nation that suffered their Vietnam ahead of ours. It also may be important to know if the book was written in 1958, before we got deeply involved, or in 1978, when the war was over. The table of contents, the preface, bibliographical notes at the end, and the index are all clues that may help us unlock the meaning of the book.

Reading Uncritically

The more difficult the text, the more important it is that we read it *uncritically* first. This doesn't seem to make sense until you realize that if the subject matter, the form of writing, and the author's style are all strange to the reader, then the reader may bog down in paying too close attention to each specific piece of information, each sentence, each word. If we pay too close attention the first time around, we have no idea of the whole, no feeling for the meaning or the purpose of the piece of writing. If we read it fast, uncritically, we will miss a lot, and at times even feel as if we were in a foreign country where we can't understand what anyone is saying. But we do pick up more than we know and get a feeling for the piece of writing. Once we have an overall view of the territory we can go back and, working within that overall vision, pay close attention to the details that will give us a true understanding of the text. Remember the first time you went to a big game; you had to try to absorb the crowd, the teams, the whole atmosphere of what was going on. You probably didn't pay too much attention to the details of the game. But when you become a fan you understand the larger context and can focus your attention on a revealing detail, such as how a player moves away from the main action of the game. Reading uncritically is the first step toward reading critically.

Reading Carefully

When a text deserves close attention, then we keep repeating the pattern of looking from larger context to smaller and back. We need to know what each word means in context, and that cannot be known simply by knowing the meaning of each word. Most words have many meanings. Those meanings change, depending on all the other meanings into which they are built. This diagram may help:

BOOK
    CHAPTER
        SECTION
            PARAGRAPH
                SENTENCE
                    PHRASE
                        WORD

It looks complicated, and it is. Reading is one of the most sophisticated, intellectual acts we perform. But remember that you bring an enormous background of experience to this task. Even if you are not a person who considers yourself a reader, you are reading other people all the time. You read your parents and your roommate, your teachers and your friends, and the strangers you meet on the street or in a bar. You read the place in which they exist—who sits behind the desk or comes around and sits beside you in a chair during an interview. You read dress—formal or casual—and whether it is appropriate to the situation and the person. We are often amused at the Freshman who tries to look middle-aged, and the middle-aged professor who tries to look like a Freshman. You read what the person says and how he or she says it. "You look as if you're new around here, can I help you?" You read body language: the hands on hips or the arms folded across the chest, or the hand extended palm out for a shake. You come to a text bringing all these intellectual skills with you so you can apply them to written language.

The diagram shows what you already do, reading the detail (the hesitant step, the avoiding eye, the move that brings the person too close to you) and fitting it into a generalization (this guy doesn't trust people like me) that, in turn, causes you to read meaning into what seemed like insignificant details a moment before. The reader moves back and forth from concept to word and word to concept, with increasing understanding. Some of the tricks of the careful reader's trade are:

Underline. It may help to understand the text if you underline key words, facts, phrases, sentences, and, on occasion, paragraphs. The purpose of underlining, however, is to help you identify the points of greatest significance and make them clear by pulling them out of the text. We have all seen inexperienced students highlighting or underlining almost every word of the text, a sure clue that they do not understand the text and are learning little from it.

Marginal Comments. Reading is a private encounter between writer and reader. Writing in the margins allows the reader to talk back—or write back—to the writer. It is a helpful way for the reader to make the text his or her own. These comments can be abrupt, quick, or extensive, sometimes even extending to a card or a piece of paper that is taped to the page. In the margin the reader agrees and disagrees, extends the text and connects it with the reader's own experience, questions the text on the basis of the reader's experience, makes connections with other experiences, other evidence, other pieces of writing. You should train yourself to become more than a passive reader, to enter into the act of making meaning with the writer.

Connecting. It is often helpful to use arrows or circles or squares or lines or numbers to connect significant facts, words, or lines in a text. Sometimes you can see the importance of a word that is repeated in a text in this way, or actually draw the map of the piece right over the text, revealing how a meaning has been woven through the text.

Outlining. The skill of outlining may be even more important to a reader than a writer. If you outline—in whatever form is comfortable to you—what is being said in the text, you will strip the text down to its essentials, and you may be able to see the meaning that lies under the text and then be able to understand what the writer was doing in the text.

Précis. This is an old-fashioned device that is extremely helpful in understanding a text. I grumped at Miss Leavitt—no Ms. in those days—who made us précis, précis, précis our way through the eleventh grade, and groaned again when I saw my English teacher for the twelfth grade—you guessed it: Miss Leavitt. I précised my way through the twelfth grade. But it taught me to read with a piercing eye, tracking down meaning and helping to teach me to write concise, disciplined prose. To write a précis, say in a few paragraphs—preferably one paragraph—what is said in an entire article, chapter, or book, using your own words. The effect of compression squeezes out the nonessentials and forces you to discover the central meaning of the text.

When we understand what the text says, then we can stand back and judge the entire text, evaluating what was said and how it was said.

Check Your Understanding

Choose the correct answer.

1. According to the author, which is not a reason that reading is so important in the modern world?
   a. Information gives the reader power in the world.
   b. Reading helps readers know and influence what is going on.
   c. Reading helps us become better writers.
   d. It helps you "read" other people more effectively.
   e. Readers can discover what they know by reading.
2. Why should you read a text uncritically at first?
   a. If you are too critical in your early reading, you may miss important details.
   b. When you read uncritically, you pay close attention to detail.
   c. By reading uncritically, you get a feeling for the reading's "atmosphere."
   d. Both *b* and *c* are correct.
   e. Both *a* and *c* are correct.
3. What should you underline or highlight when you read?
   a. almost every word of the text
   b. only key words
   c. the points of greatest importance
   d. entire paragraphs
   e. marginal comments
4. Which does not describe a précis?
   a. It is a concise summary of a reading.
   b. It is an outline of a reading.
   c. It captures the main meaning of a text.
   d. It is usually only a paragraph or two in length.
   e. It is old-fashioned.

5. What is the main difference between reading for information and reading for understanding?
   a. When you read for information, you are using the text for a specific purpose; when you read for understanding, you read to learn and make connections with the text.
   b. When you read for understanding, you learn to read better; when you read for information, you may not be "reading" at all, but gathering facts.
   c. When you read for information, you make connections between theories and ideas; when you read for understanding, you have to extract the information you need from the text.
   d. Both *a* and *c* are correct.
   e. Both *a* and *b* are correct.

6. What is the purpose of *scanning* a text?
   a. to find specific information and save time
   b. to find the index and table of contents
   c. to write an abstract of it for an academic article
   d. to read only the beginning of a text
   e. to summarize each paragraph in small type

7. Which is <u>not</u> an example of a "road sign" in a text?
   a. a chapter title
   b. a map of London
   c. the city of a book's publication
   d. a cross-head
   e. a table showing data from an experiment

8. Which of the following is the best summary sentence for this reading?
   a. Understanding the form of a text helps you understand its purpose.
   b. There are two ways to read: for understanding and for information.
   c. Reading well helps you become a better writer.
   d. Reading is a complex activity, but it is important to learn to do it well.
   e. Good readers know what they know and what they don't know when they read.

Group Discussion

Talk about these questions with your group or a partner.

1. Is reading important to you? Why or why not?
2. What is your first memory as a reader (in any language)? Why is this memory important to you?
3. What can people do to improve their reading skills?

Language Focus: Metaphors

A metaphor is a type of comparison, but one that says that something *is* something else. For example, a common metaphor is *time is a river,* in which the qualities of time are seen to have similar qualities as those of a river.

Writers use metaphors in order to create vivid images in the mind of the reader, and to create memorable ideas. (When a metaphor is overused, it becomes a *cliché.* The phrase *time is a river* is a cliché, in fact.)

The following metaphors are used in Murray's article. Can you put the underlined part of the metaphor into "plain English"? Do you think the metaphor is effective in each case? Discuss your answers with a partner or with a group.

Example: "We read for the experience of the text and we read for the information we can <u>mine</u> from it—and more." (page 16)

Meaning: get or take

Relationship between the metaphor and its meaning: To **mine** means to dig out of the earth (like mining gold). The author says "mine" instead of "get" or "take" because it gives us the image of someone **digging** for information, which is more vivid.

1. Reading stocks our mind with information and connections between pieces of information . . . ." (page 16)

   Meaning: ______________________________

   Relationship between the metaphor and its meaning: ______________

   ____

   ____

2. "If a police officer, black or white, is assigned to a neighborhood, he or she must first know what prejudices, what stereotypes, what beliefs, what fears he or she wears with the badge." (page 17)

   Meaning: ______________________________

   Relationship between the metaphor and its meaning: ______________

   ____

   ____

3. "The table of contents, the preface, bibliographical notes at the end, and the index are all clues that may help us unlock the meaning of the book." (page 19)

   Meaning: ______________________________

   Relationship between the metaphor and its meaning: ______________

   ____

   ____

4. "Once we have an overall view of the territory we can go back and, working within that overall vision, pay close attention to the details that will give us a true understanding of the text." (page 19)

   Meaning: ______________________________

   Relationship between the metaphor and its meaning: ______________

   ____

   ____

5. "Sometimes you can see the importance of a word that is repeated in a text in this way, or actually draw the map of the piece right over the text, revealing how a meaning has been woven through the text." (page 21)

   Meaning: ______________________________

   Relationship between the metaphor and its meaning: ______________

   ____

   ____

6. Write two sentences, using these words *metaphorically:* cook (verb), house (noun)

   a. ______________________________

   ____

   b. ______________________________

   ____

Chapter Wrap-Up

Speaking Activities

Class Reports

1. Meet with students who read the same reading you did. Review the questions at the end of your reading.
2. Think of one question to ask your group about the reading. Take turns asking your questions.
3. Choose someone from your group to give a report to the class. In your report, tell your classmates what you learned from your reading.
4. Teach students in other groups one important word you learned from this chapter.

Discussion

Talk about these questions with your classmates.

1. What are the qualities of a "good student," in your opinion?
2. What advice would you give to a new student at your school?
3. Why is it important to be a good reader?
4. Share some advice for studying effectively.

Writing Ideas

Think about the reading *Five Ideas to Help You Study.* Write **three more** ideas to help you study. Explain your ideas.

Read *Five Ideas to Help You Study* (page 3). Take notes on your reading using the Cornell system. Compare your notes to those written by your group members. How are your notes different? Were yours more detailed, or less detailed? How could you improve your notes?

Write a précis of the Murray article; compare it to ones written by your group members. How are your summaries different? In what way might those differences prove Murray's point about "knowing yourself" as a reader? (In other words, how does your summary reflect your own experience in life?)

Look at the Icebreaker cartoon on page 1. Write a story that tells what happened in this cartoon.

For Your Journal

Look at the photograph on page 3. Are you like the woman in the photograph? Are you organized? Neat? Describe your work habits and the place you study. Write one to two paragraphs.

CHAPTER

2 Communication

Language and Culture

Icebreaker

Discuss these questions with a partner or a group. Write down the answers.

1. Where are these people?
2. What does the woman want? What tells you that?
3. What is the man doing? What tells you that?
4. Should you raise your hand before you speak in your classes? (If you aren't sure, ask your teachers.)

CHAPTER PREVIEW

What things do you know about language and culture? Answer these questions to find out:

1. Is body language a real language? *yes* *no*
2. Can a language or culture "die"? *yes* *no*
3. Have you visited a country whose language you didn't know at all? *yes* *no*

Explain your answer: ____

____

____

____

This chapter will give you a lot of information on language and culture: body language, culture loss, and not understanding different cultures.

First Step

Vocabulary

These words on the left are in the reading. Draw a line that matches the word with its meaning. One has been done for you.

1. *communication*	a. an unhappy look
2. *facial expression*	b. the sharing of information
3. *posture*	c. a body movement
4. *gesture*	d. honest and true
5. *attitude*	e. a look on someone's face
6. *frown*	f. body position
7. *sincere*	g. an opinion or feeling

Reading

Body Language

Body language means *communication without talking.* Body language uses facial expressions, posture, and gestures. It is not a real language with words and sentences, but we can understand it. We can understand others' feelings and attitudes by watching their body language.

Body language has many different forms: facial expressions, eye contact, posture, and hand movements. It also includes how fast or how loud someone talks. Even clothing and jewelry is part of someone's body language.

Some types of body language are understood by people in all cultures. For example, certain expressions show pain in every culture. Other expressions have different meanings in different cultures. When you *nod,* or move your head up and down, this means "yes" to Americans and Europeans. However, it may mean "no" in other cultures.

Before babies can talk, they learn to control other people with body language. Of course, they do not know that they do this. For example, a parent may respond in a good way to a baby's smile. The baby may get a bad response to a frown. As a result, the baby learns to smile to get attention.

Body language also shows parts of someone's personality that he or she may want to hide. For example, someone may want to seem sincere by speaking slowly, with a lot of eye contact and a big smile. However, his or her gestures may show a different, less friendly, personality.

Spoken language—the words we say—tells others of our thoughts. Body language shows meanings and feelings that words alone cannot.

Check Your Understanding

Choose the correct answer.

1. What does *body language* mean?
   a. talking but not communicating
   b. a real language with words and sentences
   c. communicating with body movements
   d. putting clothing and jewelry on the body

2. What does the word *nod* mean?
   a. to be in pain
   b. to move your head up and down
   c. a facial expression
   d. something different in every culture

3. How can body language help us?
   a. We can understand others better.
   b. We can speak more loudly.
   c. We can speak faster.
   d. We can frown more.

4. How do babies learn body language?
   a. by frowning
   b. by nodding
   c. by controlling other people
   d. by getting good responses

5. How might someone try to look sincere to others?
   a. speaking loudly
   b. speaking softly and slowly
   c. looking someone in the eyes
   d. hiding their gestures

6. The last sentence says: "Body language shows meanings and feelings that words alone cannot." What is another way to say this sentence?
   a. Body language shows meanings and feelings that words cannot show.
   b. Body language shows meanings and feelings that words can show alone.
   c. Body language shows meanings and feelings; words can't show meanings or feelings.
   d. Body language shows meanings and feelings that words cannot show by themselves.

Group Discussion

Talk about these questions with your group or a partner.

1. What kind of body language shows someone is friendly?
2. What kind of body language might show you are a good student?
3. Do you find others' body language interesting? Why or why not?

Language Focus: *by + doing*

In the reading, you will see this sentence:

> We can understand others' feelings and attitudes **by watching** their body language.

The phrase *by doing* something tells us *how* something is done. Complete the sentences below with a *by* ____+ *ing* phrase. Choose a base word from the list below:

~~*move*~~ *frown* *speak* *wear* *smile* *use*

Example: Europeans might say yes __by moving__ their heads up and down.

1. A baby may show happiness to her parents ______________.
2. We communicate with our bodies ______________ postures and gestures.
3. We can show unhappiness ______________.
4. Someone may seem sincere ______________ slowly.
5. A person might express herself ______________ jewelry.

6. Write two more sentences using the *by* + *doing* phrase:

   a. ____

   ____

   b. ____

   ____

Second Step

Vocabulary

These words are in the reading. Do you know what they mean? Discuss the meaning of these words with a classmate or your teacher. Write the meanings in the spaces.

1. *heritage:* ____

   ____

2. *comeback:* ____

   ____

3. *decree:* ____

   ____

4. *purification:* ____

   ____

5. *holocaust:* ____

   ____

6. *pagan:* ____

   ____

7. *sapling:* ____

   ____

8. *haunt:* ______________________________

____

9. *traumatic:* ______________________________

____

10. *powwow:* ______________________________

____

Reading

Reading Note: *The Ojibwa are an American Indian nation located around the upper Great Lakes in both Canada and the United States.*

The Road Back

by Deanna Weniger

About the Author: Deanna Weniger is an award-winning author for the Port Huron Times Herald. *She writes a regular column for the newspaper about local and international topics.*

Teresa Altiman makes a determined effort to weave her ancient heritage into her modern life.

She greets kids at the Walpole Island Children's Center with an enthusiastic "*Boozhoo!,*" or *hello,* and often interchanges English and Ojibwa terms in conversation.

She is not fluent in the native language, although she wants to be.

Perhaps it comes naturally, as she is the center's cultural-enrichment instructor. Or perhaps she's part of a growing trend of natives working hard to reconnect with their Indian culture.

"Things that were slipping away—I see coming back," she said. "A few of us just now are trying to relearn our language."

Other traditions, such as the sweat-lodge ceremony, drumming, chanting and dancing, once forbidden either by law or Christian influence, also are making a comeback, she said.

Lynette Isaac, 24, said her search to understand her people's past helps complete her spiritually.

"I just feel whole as a person, knowing my beliefs and my traditions are there," she said.

Cultural Holocaust

It's difficult to look at any aspect of Walpole Island without running into stories about residential schools.

In the early to mid-1900s, the Canadian government decreed it legal for Indian children to be taken from their homes to be educated in Ontario schools.

"I would say 'holocaust' in referring to what the residential schools did to our culture," Altiman said.

Her parents were taken. As a result, they lost their language and culture and were unable to pass that heritage on to their children.

"They drove it out of me when I went to school," remembers Jasper John, 78, who was taken at age 7. "It was tough up there."

His wife, Eliza, 64, remembers her parents being secretive about attending ceremonies, such as the sweat-lodge purification ceremony. The Anglican Church, which had converted many Indians to Christianity, frowned on those traditions as pagan.

In the sweat-lodge ceremony, water is poured over hot stones inside a dome-shaped structure made from saplings. Sweat runs down the body and takes the poisons out. The Great Spirit is invited in, and participants ask forgiveness for wrongdoing.

Eliza John is one of 30 remaining island natives who can speak fluent Ojibwa. She said young people often come to her with questions about their culture.

Ojibwa Sweat Lodge, 1932

Traditions Returning

Depression, poverty and all the ugly things that haunt the adults who had traumatic childhoods in the residential schools carried over into the next generation.

"There was alcoholism, there was abuse," Isaac said. "My grandmother went to the residential school, and she would not speak her language."

But Isaac sees hope for renewal in the eyes of her three young children. "For my generation, I think that cycle will be broken," she said.

She has taken up hand drumming and works to expose her children to cultural events.

"I'm trying to learn the language with some of the songs

that we're singing," she said. "I take my children to traditional ceremonies. I have not been in a sweat lodge, but my boys have."

Island leaders are advertising for a language coordinator who could run a language center and present programs in Ojibwa to help promote the culture.

Because this generation did not grow up with many Indian traditions, rediscovering their heritage will take work.

"I wanted to start learning about the culture that I didn't have," said Stacey Nahdee, 35, while taking a break at a June powwow from singing and striking a cedar shell drum capped with buffalo hide.

"I didn't grow up with this," Nahdee said. "I'm choosing to do this as a result of changing my own life."

Check Your Understanding

Write short answers to the questions below. Check your answers with your group or a partner.

1. Who are the Ojibwa?

____

____

2. Describe the sweat-lodge ceremony in your own words.

____

____

3. Explain what the Canadian residential schools were.

____

____

4. What was the effect of the residential schools on the Ojibwa?

____

____

5. Why will it be hard for many Ojibwa people to discover their heritage?

____

____

Group Discussion

Talk about these questions with your group or a partner.

1. What do you know about Native Americans (First Nations people)? How did you learn what you know?
2. In your opinion, why did the Canadian government separate families of the native people?
3. What might parents do to help their children keep their culture?

Language Focus: Specialized Vocabulary

When you read in a new academic area, you will often find specialized vocabulary to talk about that area. In this article, the topic is Native Americans, or First Nations people. When you study the vocabulary that is special to the topic, you begin to understand it better.

Here are the words or phrases that are related to this topic. Be sure you understand all of them.

1. *buffalo hide*
2. *cedar shell drum*
3. *chanting*
4. *dancing*
5. *drumming*
6. *heritage*
7. *native language*
8. *Ojibwa*
9. *powwow*
10. *purification ceremony*
11. *residential schools*
12. *sweat-lodge ceremony*
13. *the Great Spirit*
14. *tradition*

Write five sentences in which you show the connection between at least two of the items on the list in each sentence. For example, using *Ojibwa* and *residential schools,* you might write:

Example: The older Ojibwa people were separated from their families and sent to residential schools.

1. ______________________________

2. ______________________________

3. ______________________________

4. ______________________________

5. ______________________________

Third Step

Vocabulary

This reading has many words you may not know. Check off the ones you are sure you do know. Look up the others, and write a short definition in your own words beside it.

- ☐ *memorial* (noun): ______________________________
- ☐ *pagoda:* ______________________________

- ☐ *Shinto shrine:* ____________________

____

- ☐ *bamboo grove:* ____________________

____

- ☐ *nightingale:* ____________________

____

- ☐ *fathom* (verb): ____________________

____

- ☐ *corps de ballet:* ____________________

____

- ☐ *brazenly:* ____________________

____

- ☐ *swelter:* ____________________

____

- ☐ *coed:* ____________________

____

- ☐ *avert:* ____________________

____

- ☐ *mortify:* ____________________

____

- ☐ *transgression:* ____________________

____

- ☐ *spew:* ____________________

____

☐ *wail:* ____

____

☐ *blight:* ____

____

☐ *baleful:* ____

____

☐ *terra cognita:* ____

____

☐ *abject:* ____

____

☐ *buffet* (verb): ____

____

Reading

Reading Note: *It's not important to know what an abacus, a bathysphere, a conundrum, a diatribe, or an eggplant is in order to understand the first paragraph. Think instead about the rules of the "game" the writer is describing.*

Going to Japan

by Barbara Kingsolver

About the Author: Barbara Kingsolver was born in 1955 in Kentucky. She graduated from Depauw University in Indiana and lived in Europe for awhile, working in different jobs. She has written many very popular books, including The Bean Trees *and* The Poisonwood Bible. *She lives in Tucson, Arizona, with her family. This essay was published in 1994, but she first told the story in 1992 in a speech.*

My great-aunt Zelda went to Japan and took an abacus, a bathysphere, a conundrum, a diatribe, an eggplant. That was a game we used to play. All you had to do was remember everything in alphabetical order. Right up to Aunt Zelda.

Then I grew up and was actually invited to go to Japan, not with the fantastic Aunt Zelda but as myself. As such, I had no idea what to take. I knew what I planned to be doing: researching a story about the memorial at Hiroshima; visiting friends; trying not to get lost in a place where I couldn't even read the street signs. Times being what they were—*any* times—I intended to do my very best to respect cultural differences, avoid sensitive topics I might not comprehend, and, in short, be anything but an Ugly American.* When I travel, I like to try to blend in. I've generally found it helps to be prepared. So I asked around, and was warned to expect a surprisingly modern place.

My great-aunt Zelda went to Japan and took Appliances, Battery packs, Cellular technology . . . . That seemed to be the idea.

And so it came to pass that I arrived in Kyoto an utter foreigner, unprepared. It's true that there are electric streetcars there, and space-age gas stations with uniformed attendants who rush to

* "Ugly American" is a reference to a 1958 book by William Lederer. It portrayed American political policy in Asia in an uncomplimentary fashion.

help you from all directions at once. There are also golden pagodas on shimmering lakes, and Shinto shrines in the forests. There are bamboo groves and nightingales. And finally there are more invisible guidelines for politeness than I could fathom. When I stepped on a streetcar, a full head taller than all the other passengers, I became an awkward giant. I took up too much space. I blended in like Igor would blend in with the corps de ballet in *Swan Lake.* I bumped into people. I crossed my arms when I listened, which turns out to be, in Japanese body language, the sign for indicating brazenly that one is bored.

But I wasn't! I was struggling through my days and nights in the grip of boredom's opposite—i.e., panic. I didn't know how to eat noodle soup with chopsticks, and I did it most picturesquely *wrong.* I didn't know how to order, so I politely deferred to my hosts and more than once was served a cuisine with heads, including eyeballs. I managed to wrestle these creatures to my lips with chopsticks, but it was already too late by the time I got the message that *one does not spit out anything.*

I undertook this trip in high summer, when it is surprisingly humid and warm in southern Japan. I never imagined that in such sweltering heat women would be expected to wear stockings, but every woman in Kyoto wore nylon stockings. Coeds in shorts *on the tennis court* wore nylon stockings. I had packed only skirts and sandals; people averted their eyes.

When I went to Japan I took my Altitude, my Bare-naked legs, my Callous foreign ways. I was mortified.

My hosts explained to me that the Japanese language does not accommodate insults, only infinite degrees of apology. I quickly memorized an urgent one, "*Sumimasen,*" and another for especially extreme cases, "*Moshi wake gozaimasen.*" This translates approximately to mean, "If you please, my transgression is so inexcusable that I wish I were dead."

I needed these words. When I touched the outside surface of a palace wall, curious to know what it was made of, I set off screeching alarms and a police car came scooting up the lawn's discreet gravel path. "*Moshi wake gozaimasen,* Officer! Wish I were dead!" And in the public bath, try as I might, I couldn't get the hang of showering with a hand-held nozzle while sitting fourteen inches from a stranger. I sprayed my elderly neighbor with cold water. In the face.

"*Moshi wake gozaimasen,*" I declared, with feeling.

She merely stared, dismayed by the foreign menace.

I visited a Japanese friend, and in her small, perfect house I spewed out my misery. "Everything I do is wrong!" I wailed like a child. "I'm a blight on your country."

"Oh, no," she said calmly. "To forgive, for us, is the highest satisfaction. To forgive a foreigner, ah! Even better." She smiled. "You have probably made many people happy here."

To stomp about the world ignoring cultural differences is arrogant, to be sure, but perhaps there is another kind of arrogance in the presumption that we may ever really build a faultless bridge from one shore to another, or even know where the mist has ceded to landfall. When I finally arrived at Ground Zero in Hiroshima, I stood speechless. What I found there was a vast and exquisitely silent monument to forgiveness. I was moved beyond words, even beyond tears, to think of all that can be lost or gained in the gulf between any act of will and its consequences. In the course of every failure of understanding, we have so much to learn.

I remembered my Japanese friend's insistence on forgiveness as the highest satisfaction, and I understood it really for the first time: What a rich wisdom it would be, and how much more bountiful a harvest, to gain pleasure not from achieving personal perfection but from understanding the inevitability of imperfection and pardoning those who also fall short of it.

I have walked among men and made mistakes without number. When I went to Japan I took my Abject goodwill, my Baleful excuses, my Cringing remorse. I couldn't remember everything, could not even recite the proper alphabet. So I gave myself away instead, evidently as a kind of public service. I prepared to return home feeling empty-handed.

At the Osaka Airport I sat in my plane on the runway, waiting to leave for terra cognita, as the aircraft's steel walls were buffeted by the sleet and winds of a typhoon. We waited for an hour, then longer, with no official word from the cockpit, and then suddenly our flight was canceled. Air traffic control in Tokyo had been struck by lightning; no flights possible until the following day.

"We are so sorry," the pilot told us. "You will be taken to a hotel, fed, and brought back here for your flight tomorrow. " As we passengers rose slowly and disembarked, we were met by an airline official who had been posted in the exit port for the sole purpose of saying to each and every one of us, "Terrible, terrible. *Sumimasen.*" Other travelers nodded indifferently, but not me. I took the startled gentleman by the hands and practically kissed him.

"You have no idea," I told him, "how thoroughly I forgive you."

Check Your Understanding

Write short answers to the questions below. Check your answers with your group or a partner.

1. Why did Barbara Kingsolver go to Japan?

 ____

 ____

2. What problems did she encounter there?

 ____

 ____

3. What was Kingsolver's attitude about Japanese culture?

 ____

 ____

4. What mistake in body language did Kingsolver make?

 ____

 ____

5. Explain Kingsolver's reaction to the Hiroshima monument. Why does she call it a "monument to forgiveness"?

 ____

 ____

6. Why does Kingsolver "forgive" the airline official of her canceled flight?

 ____

 ____

Group Discussion

Talk about these questions with your group or a partner.

1. Why did Kingsolver write this article, do you think?
2. Identify one or two sentences in the reading that you particularly like. Read them to your group members, and explain why you chose them.
3. Do you enjoy reading about travel adventures? Have you read any others you would like others to know about? Explain your answer.

Language Focus: Idioms

This story contains several idioms, or phrases with particular meanings. Can you rewrite the sentences, changing the underlined text into non-idiomatic language? Work with a partner or small group.

Example: Times being what they were, I intended to respect cultural differences.

Because of the situation at that time in history,
I intended to respect cultural differences.

1. I like to try to blend in when I travel.

____

____

2. I asked around to find out more about Japan.

____

____

3. I was a full head taller than all the other passengers.

____

____

4. I couldn't get the hang of showering with a hand-held nozzle.

5. I crossed my arms when I listened, which turns out to be the sign for showing boredom.

6. And so it came to pass that I arrived in Kyoto an utter foreigner, unprepared.

7. Choose one of the underlined idioms and write a sentence about yourself.

Chapter Wrap-Up

Speaking Activities

Class Reports

1. Meet with students who read the same reading you did. Review the questions at the end of the reading.
2. Think of one question to ask your group about the reading. Take turns asking your questions.
3. Choose someone from your group to give a report to the class. In your report, tell your classmates what you learned from your reading.
4. Teach students in other groups one important word you learned from this chapter.

Discussion

1. Demonstrate one body language gesture (polite ones only, please!) and explain what it means.
2. Have you ever visited a culture you didn't understand? What happened?
3. When you travel, do you like to *blend in* or *stand out?* Explain your answer.
4. Is it important for a group to keep its old ways? Or, should it just adjust to the modern world? Explain your answer.
5. Can a group keep its culture if it loses its language? Explain your answer.
6. Here are the rules of the game described in *Going to Japan:*
    1. The first person says, "I'm going on a trip and I'm taking a ________________." The item has to begin with an "A," such as an apple.
    2. The second person says, "I'm going on a trip and I'm taking an apple, and a ________________. That item has to begin with a "B."
    3. The third person has to repeat the entire statement, and add an item that begins with "C," and so forth through the alphabet. The first person to make a mistake is out of the game.
    4. The game starts again with "A" with the next person, and repeats the steps above.
    5. The person who never forgets wins the game.

With your class or a group, play Going on a Trip.

Writing Ideas

Go to a public place, like a café or shop. Watch some of the people there. Write down one or two kinds of body language you see. Write a paragraph to explain what the body language means.

Write two paragraphs summarizing *The Road Back.* Compare your summary to a classmate's. What details did you keep? Which did your classmate keep? How can you improve your summary?

Barbara Kingsolver says, "What a rich wisdom it would be, and how much more bountiful a harvest, to gain pleasure not from achieving personal perfection but from understanding the inevitability of imperfection and pardoning those who also fall short of it." Do you agree with this statement? Write two to three paragraphs in which you explain this statement, and explain why you agree or disagree with it.

You are learning English. In writing, explain why this is important to you. Also explain why your first language, or other languages, are important, too.

For Your Journal

Have you ever felt "out of place"? Write about any experience you have had like this. For example, perhaps you visited another country, or started a new job. How did you feel? Why is that experience memorable to you?

CHAPTER

3 Education

Genius

Icebreaker

Albert Einstein in Berlin, Germany

Discuss these questions with a partner or a group. Write down the answers to report to your group or to the class.

1. Where did you go to school?
2. What is the meaning of the word *genius?* Who is a genius?
3. How much do you know about Albert Einstein? Explain your answer.

CHAPTER PREVIEW

What things do you know about education and genius? Answer these questions to find out:

1. Do you know who Helen Keller was? *yes* *no*
2. Did you see the movie *A Beautiful Mind?* *yes* *no*
3. Do you know who Malcolm X was? *yes* *no*

Explain your answer: ____________________

____

____

____

This chapter presents the stories of three famous people in education: Helen Keller, John Nash, and Malcolm X.

First Step

Vocabulary

These words are in the reading. Match each word to its meaning. Draw a line to the correct answer.

1. *imitate*	a. movement
2. *mug*	b. cleaned off; brushed dirt away
3. *confused*	c. pleased and satisfied
4. *spout*	d. mixed up
5. *swept*	e. place where water comes out
6. *motion*	f. to copy or try to be like
7. *proud*	g. secrecy; unknown things
8. *mystery*	h. a type of cup

Reading

My Teacher Arrives

Adapted from *The Story of My Life*
by Helen Keller

About the Author: Helen Keller was born June 27, 1880, in Alabama. When she was 19 months old, Keller had a fever that made her blind and deaf. Her teacher, Anne Sullivan, taught Keller to read, write, and speak. Keller spent the rest of her life working to improve the quality of life for disabled people.

The most important day I remember in all my life is when my teacher, Anne Mansfield Sullivan, arrived. It was March 3, 1887, three months before I was seven years old.

That afternoon, I waited on the porch. Something unusual was going to happen, so I waited on the steps. The afternoon sun fell on my face. I did not know what the future held for me. I had been angry and sad for weeks.

I felt footsteps coming, and I stretched out my hand to my mother. Someone took it, and I was picked up and held in the arms of my teacher,

Helen Keller and Anne Sullivan

Miss Annie Sullivan. She was there to teach me everything, and, above all, to love me.

The next morning, my teacher took me into her room and gave me a doll. After I played with it a little while, Miss Sullivan slowly spelled into my hand the word *"d-o-l-l."* I tried to imitate her fingers. I finally succeeded in making the letters right; I was happy and proud of myself. I ran downstairs to my mother and held up my hand and made the letters for *doll.* I did not know I was spelling a word. I didn't know what words were. After that, I learned to spell a lot of words, like *pin, hat, cup* and a few verbs like *sit, stand* and *walk.* But it was several weeks before I understood that everything has a name.

One day, while I was playing with my new doll, Miss Sullivan put another doll into my lap, and spelled *"d-o-l-l."* She wanted me to understand that *"d-o-l-l"* was the name for both toys. Earlier that day, I couldn't understand the words *"m-u-g"* and *"w-a-t-e-r."* Miss Sullivan tried to teach me that *"m-u-g"* is mug and that *"w-a-t-e-r"* is water, but I confused the two. I got angry and threw the new doll on the floor. I was happy when I felt the pieces of the broken doll at my feet. I wasn't sorry because I didn't love the doll. In my quiet, dark world, I had no strong feelings. My teacher swept the pieces up, and I was happy the doll was gone. She brought me my hat.

We walked down the path to the well house. My teacher placed my hand under the spout. As the cool stream spilled over one hand, she spelled the word *water* into the other, first slowly, then quickly. I felt the motion of her fingers. Suddenly I understood the mystery of language. I knew that *"w-a-t-e-r"* was the wonderful cool thing on my hand. That word awakened my soul, gave it light, hope, joy, set it free!

I left the well-house eager to learn. Everything had a name, and each name gave me a new thought. We returned to the house, where every object I touched came alive. I remembered the doll I had broken. I found it and picked up the pieces. I tried to put them together. Then my eyes filled with tears because I knew what I had done, and for the first time I felt sadness.

I learned many new words that day. I do not remember them all, but some of them were: *mother, father, sister,* and *teacher.* These words made the world come alive for me. I was the happiest child in the world that day. I remembered the joys the day had brought me. For the first time, I wanted a new day to come.

Check Your Understanding

Mark *true* or *false* for each question.

1. Anne Sullivan was Helen Keller's mother.

   true *false*

2. Helen Keller was three months old when Anne arrived.

   true *false*

3. Helen Keller learned to spell using her fingers.

   true *false*

4. Anne Sullivan broke Helen's doll because she was angry.

   true *false*

5. *Water* was the first word that Helen really understood.

   true *false*

Group Discussion

Talk about these questions with your group or a partner.

1. Why was Helen "angry and sad" for so long?
2. What kind of teacher was Anne Sullivan?
3. Why did Helen break her doll?
4. Why was water important to Helen?

Language Focus: Preposition Practice

Choose one of the prepositions to complete each sentence.

for *in* *of* *on* *to*

Example: I waited __on__ the steps.

1. Doll was the name ________ the toy.
2. I felt the water ________ the back of my hand.
3. I had been angry ________ weeks.
4. I succeeded ________ doing it right.
5. I was proud ________ myself because I spelled it correctly.
6. I was the happiest child ________ the world.
7. My teacher held me ________ her arms.
8. The sun fell ________ my face.
9. We walked down the path ________ the well house.
10. What did the future hold ________ me?

Second Step

Vocabulary

These words are found in the reading. Check the ones you know. Write a short definition for each.

☐ *schizophrenia:* ______________________

____

☐ *scholar:* ______________________

____

☐ *daunting:* ______________________

____

☐ *haunt:* ______________________

____

☐ *stunned:* ______________________

____

☐ *nominations:* ______________________

____

☐ *substantial:* ______________________

____

☐ *podium:* ______________________

____

☐ *squawk:* ______________________

____

☐ *indulge:* ______________________

____

Reading

A Beautiful Mind

The movie *A Beautiful Mind* was inspired by the life of John Forbes Nash, Jr., and was partly based on the biography *A Beautiful Mind* by Sylvia Nasar. John Nash was born in West Virginia, June 13, 1928. He was well known in "new mathematics" in the 1950s, but he seemed to disappear when schizophrenia affected his life. By 1994, Nash had gained control of his illness and was working again as a scholar. That year, he received the Nobel Prize in Economic Science.

The following scenes take place at the end of the movie. In the first, Nash has returned to Princeton University after dealing with mental illness. Nash has been told he will receive the Nobel Prize, and then he receives the prize in Sweden. (Martin Hansen is a professor at Princeton; Alicia is Nash's wife; King is part of the Nobel Committee.)

Nash: I was thinking I might teach.

Hansen: A classroom with fifty students is daunting for anyone. And you're a terrible teacher, John.

Nash: Details, details.

Hansen: What about, you know . . . Are they gone?

Nash: Oh no, they're not gone. Maybe they will never be. But I've gotten used to ignoring them. And I think, as a result, they've kind of given up on me. Do you think that's the way it is with our dreams and our nightmares? That we have to keep feeding them for them to stay alive?

Hansen: But they haunt you?

Nash: They're my past, Martin. Everybody is haunted by their past. Do you understand?

Hansen: Maybe. Almost.

Nash: I've got to go. Alicia still worries if I'm late. You get a lot of attention when you're crazy.

Hansen: I'll talk to the department. Maybe in the spring. Hey Nash, you scared?

* * *

King: Professor, my name is Thomas King. I am here to tell you that you are being considered for the Nobel Prize.

Nash: I'm sorry. I'm just a bit stunned.

King: Over the last ten years your work in game theory* has become the foundation of modern economics.

Nash: Suddenly everybody likes that one. What about my work on manifold embedding?

King: Your equilibrium's applications to FCC bandwidth auctions, to anti-trust cases . . .

Nash: Anti-trust cases? Huh? I never would have thought of that.

King: Shall we have some tea?

Nash: I don't really go in there. I usually just take a sandwich in the library . . . Things have changed. I thought the nominations for the Nobel Prize were a secret. I thought you only knew if you won or lost.

King: That is generally the case, yes. But these are special circumstances. The awards are substantial. They require private funding. As such, the image of the Nobel is quite important.

Nash: So you came here to see if I was crazy. To see if I'd screw everything up if I actually won. Maybe dance at the podium or strip naked and squawk like a chicken.

King: Something like that, yes.

Nash: Would I embarrass you? Yes, I suppose it's possible. You see, I am crazy. I take the newer medications. I still see things that are not here. But I choose

* This line and the next five lines of text contain mathematical terms that are not important to understand. The writer is showing how complex Nash's ideas are.

to ignore them. Like a diet of the mind. I do not indulge certain appetites. My appetite for patterns, and perhaps my appetite to imagine, even to dream. I have lost much.

* * *

Nash: Thank you. Thank you for your patience. I have always believed in numbers, in the equations and logics that lead to reason. I was wrong. It is only in the mysterious equations of love that any logic or reason can be found. Perhaps it is good to have a beautiful mind. But a better gift is to discover a beautiful heart. Thank you for your belief in me after so many years. You are the reason I am here today. You are the reason I am. Thank you.

Check Your Understanding

Choose the correct answer.

1. When did Nash receive the Nobel Prize?
   a. 1928
   b. 1950
   c. 1994
   d. 1956
2. What disease did Nash suffer from?
   a. equilibrium
   b. schizophrenia
   c. manifold embedding
   d. nightmares
3. Hansen asks Nash, “Are they gone?” Who is he talking about?
   a. Nash’s students
   b. Nash’s family
   c. the details
   d. imaginary people

4. Why does Alicia worry when Nash is late?
   a. She has nightmares.
   b. She has given up on him.
   c. He has been ill.
   d. He ignores her.

5. Why does Mr. King visit Nash?
   a. to tell him he might win the Nobel Prize
   b. to invite him to teach at Princeton
   c. to tell him he has won the Nobel Prize
   d. to discuss economic theory with him

6. What was unusual about Mr. King's visit?
   a. He wouldn't tell Nash if he'd won or lost.
   b. He was asking for private funding.
   c. He ate lunch in the library.
   d. Usually, nominations were a secret.

7. What did Nash say in his speech?
   a. It is most important to be smart and logical.
   b. It is better to have a good heart than reason.
   c. Solving equations is a mysterious process.
   d. He was wrong to discover equations and logic.

Group Discussion

Talk about these questions with your group or a partner.

1. Why was Mr. King worried about Nash's receiving the Nobel Prize?
2. Do you agree with Nash's speech about a "beautiful mind"?
3. The Nobel Prize is an important academic award. What other prizes do you know about? What prize would you like to earn? Why?

Language Focus: Sentence Fragments

Sentence fragments are sentences that do not contain both a subject and a verb. Although in writing they are often considered ungrammatical, in fact, sentence fragments are used frequently in spoken language.

The following are sentence fragments from the reading. Find them in the reading and then rewrite them, using the information found in the reading to complete the sentence.

Example: That we have to keep feeding them for them to stay alive?

Do we have to keep feeding our dreams and nightmares for them to stay alive?

1. Maybe in the spring. ____________________

____

2. Hey Nash, you scared? ____________________

____

3. To see if I'd screw everything up if I actually won.

____

____

4. Maybe dance at the podium or strip naked and squawk like a chicken.

____

____

5. Like a diet of the mind. ____________________

____

6. My appetite for patterns, and perhaps my appetite to imagine, even to dream.

____

____

Third Step

Vocabulary

These words are in the reading. Find them in an English-English dictionary. Discuss their definition with a classmate or your teacher. Write the meanings, and in your own words, write a sample sentence that shows you understand the meaning. (See page 12 for an example.)

1. *emulate:* ______________________________

   ____

   Sample sentence: ______________________________

   ____

2. *penmanship:* ______________________________

   ____

   Sample sentence: ______________________________

   ____

3. *riffling:* ______________________________

   ____

   Sample sentence: ______________________________

   ____

4. *painstaking:* ______________________________

   ____

   Sample sentence: ______________________________

   ____

5. *burrowing:* ______________________________

____

Sample sentence: ______________________________

____

6. *termites:* ______________________________

____

Sample sentence: ______________________________

____

Reading

Prison Studies

by Malcolm X

About the Author: Malcolm X was born Malcolm Little in Omaha, Nebraska, on May 19, 1925. He had a difficult and unhappy childhood. His father was murdered, and his mother was institutionalized with mental illness. Malcolm became involved with crime and eventually ended up in jail. In prison, he began a process of self-education and eventually became one of the United States' best-known fighters for civil rights for African Americans. He was assassinated in 1965.

Many who today hear me somewhere in person, or on television, or those who read something I've said, will think I went to school far beyond the eighth grade. This impression is due entirely to my prison studies.

It had really begun back in the Charlestown Prison, when Bimbi first made me feel envy of his stock of knowledge. Bimbi had

aard·vark (ärd värk) *n.*
A burrowing mammal *(Orycteropus afer)* of southern Africa, having a stocky, hairy body, large ears, a long tubular snout, and powerful digging claws.

Source: Dictionary.com

always taken charge of any conversation he was in, and I had tried to emulate him. But every book I picked up had few sentences which didn't contain anywhere from one to nearly all of the words that might as well have been in Chinese. When I just skipped those words, of course, I really ended up with little idea of what the book said. So I had come to the Norfolk Prison Colony still going through only book-reading motions. Pretty soon, I would have quit even these motions, unless I had received the motivation that I did.

I saw that the best thing I could do was get hold of a dictionary—to study, to learn some words. I was lucky enough to reason also that I should try to improve my penmanship. It was sad. I couldn't even write in a straight line. It was both ideas together that moved me to request a dictionary along with some tablets and pencils from the Norfolk Prison Colony school.

I spent two days just riffling uncertainly through the dictionary's pages. I'd never realized so many words existed! I didn't know which words I needed to learn. Finally, to start some kind of action, I began copying.

In my slow, painstaking, ragged handwriting, I copied into my tablet everything printed on that first page, down to the punctuation marks.

I believe it took me a day. Then, aloud, I read back, to myself, everything I'd written on the tablet. Over and over, aloud, to myself, I read my own handwriting.

I woke up the next morning, thinking about those words—immensely proud to realize that not only had I written so much at one time, but I'd written words that I never knew were in the world. Moreover, with a little effort, I also could remember what many of these words meant. I reviewed the words whose meanings I didn't remember. Funny thing, from the dictionary's first page right now, that "aardvark" springs to my mind. The dictionary had a picture of it, a long-tailed, long-eared, burrowing African mammal, which lives off termites caught by sticking out its tongue as an anteater does for ants.

I was so fascinated that I went on—I copied the dictionary's next page. And the same experience came when I studied that. With every succeeding page, I also learned of people and places and events from history. Actually the dictionary is like a miniature encyclopedia. Finally the dictionary's A section had filled a whole tablet—and I went on into the B's. That was the way I started copying what eventually became the entire dictionary. It went a lot faster after so much practice helped me to pick up handwriting speed. Between what I wrote in my tablet, and writing letters, during the rest of my time in prison I would guess I wrote a million words.

I suppose it was inevitable that as my word-base broadened, I could for the first time pick up a book and read and now begin to understand what the book was saying. Anyone who has read a great deal can imagine the new world that opened. Let me tell you something; from then until I left that prison, in every free moment I had, if I was not reading in the library, I was reading on my bunk. You couldn't have gotten me out of books with a wedge. Between Mr. Muhammad's teachings, my correspondence, my visitors—usually Ella and Reginald—and my reading of books, months passed without my even thinking about being imprisoned. In fact, up to then, I never had been so truly free in my life.

Check Your Understanding

Write short answers to the following questions. Check your answers with a partner or with your group.

1. When did Malcolm X's formal education end?

____

____

2. What does the author mean when he says he was "going through only book-reading motions"?

____

____

3. What role did the dictionary play in his prison education?

____

____

4. Why does Malcolm X say that he "had never been so truly free" in his life, even though he was in prison?

____

____

Group Discussion

Talk about these questions with your group or a partner.

1. Do you think that Malcolm X's educational method would work for you? Why or why not?
2. Why was the word *aardvark* symbolic to Malcolm X, in your opinion?
3. Has the dictionary been an important tool in your English learning? How can you make good use of a dictionary?

Language Focus: Understanding Complex Sentences

These sentences are found in the reading. Rewrite them in your own words, showing you understand what they mean. Focus particularly on the underlined parts.

1. It had really begun back in the Charlestown Prison, when Bimbi first <u>made me feel envy of his stock of knowledge</u>.

____

____

2. In my <u>slow, painstaking, ragged</u> handwriting, I copied into my tablet everything printed on that first page, <u>down to the punctuation marks</u>.

____

____

3. Funny thing, from the dictionary's first page right now, that "aardvark" springs to my mind.

4. With every succeeding page, I also learned of people and places and events from history.

5. I suppose it was inevitable that as my word-base broadened, I could for the first time pick up a book and read and now begin to understand what the book was saying.

6. You couldn't have gotten me out of books with a wedge.

Chapter Wrap-Up

Speaking Activities

Class Reports

1. Meet with students who read the same reading you did. Review the questions at the end of the reading.
2. Think of one question to ask your group about the reading. Take turns asking your questions.
3. Do some additional research about the person in your reading. Check the Internet or your library for more information.

4. Choose someone from your group to give a report to the class. In your report, tell your classmates what you learned from your reading and your research.
5. Teach students in other groups one important word you learned from this chapter.

Discussion

1. Is it more important to learn from books or from experience? Explain your answer.
2. Helen Keller had physical handicaps. John Nash suffered from mental illness. Malcolm X had a violent and unhappy childhood. Do you think these things affected their educations? How?
3. Who in the world today do you consider very smart? What makes this person smart?

Writing Ideas

At the end of the reading, Helen Keller says, "For the first time, I wanted a new day to come." Why does she say this? Write one or two paragraphs explaining your answer.

In your opinion, what does it mean to have a "beautiful mind"? Explain your answer in two to three paragraphs.

Irony is when things happen that don't match our expectations. In what way is Malcolm X's story *ironic?* Explain your answer.

From the research you did for your class discussion, write a short biography (two to three paragraphs) about the person featured in your reading.

For Your Journal

All of the readings in the chapter focus on education, genius, and difficult challenges. What challenges have you faced in your education? How have you overcome these challenges?

CHAPTER

4 English

American Short Stories

Icebreaker

Discuss these questions with a partner or a group. Write down the answers.

1. Do you know the story represented in this picture? What is it? Tell your partner or group members.
2. What's the last movie you saw? What story did it tell?
3. Tell a story of something funny that happened to you.

CHAPTER PREVIEW

What things do you know about reading short stories? Answer these questions to find out:

1. Do you know what a *fable* is? *yes* *no*
2. Have you heard of the writer Ray Bradbury? *yes* *no*
3. Have you read stories about people from different cultures? *yes* *no*

Explain your answer: ____________________

____

____

____

This chapter presents three famous American short stories.

First Step

Vocabulary

This reading has many words you may not know. Check off the ones you know. Look up the others, and write their meanings in your own words beside it.

☐ *fable:* ____________________

____

☐ *clean-shaven:* ____________________

____

☐ *slightly:* ____________________

____

☐ *exactly:* ____________________

____

☐ *envying:* ____________________

____

☐ *attracted:* ____________________

____

☐ *staring:* ____________________

____

☐ *district:* ____________________

____

☐ *opposite:* ____________________

____

☐ *pretext:* ____________________

____

☐ *vacated:* ____________________

____

☐ *warning:* ____________________

____

☐ *drowned out:* ____________________

____

☐ *wrinkled:* ____________________

____

☐ *applauded:* ____________________

____

☐ *expected:* ______________________________

____

☐ *conductor:* ______________________________

____

☐ *solemn:* ______________________________

____

Reading

Reading Note: *When you read the story, don't stop to look up words.*

A Fable

by Robert Fox

About the Author: Robert Fox lives in Columbus, Ohio. In 1988, he published Tlar & Codpol: The Last American Revolution/Confessions of Dead Politicians *(two novels) (December Press). Fox is the literature program coordinator for the Ohio Arts Council and the founder of Carpenter Press. He is also a blues musician.*

The young man was clean-shaven and neatly dressed. It was early Monday morning and he got on the subway. It was the first day of his first job and he was slightly nervous; he didn't know exactly what his job would be. Otherwise he felt fine. He loved everybody he saw. He loved everybody on the street and everybody disappearing into the subway, and he loved the world because it was a fine clear day and he was starting his first job.

Without kicking anybody, the young man was able to find a seat on the Manhattan-bound train. The car filled quickly and he looked up at the people standing over him envying his seat. Among them were a mother and daughter who were going shopping. The daughter was a beautiful girl with blond hair and soft-looking skin, and he was immediately attracted to her.

"He's staring at you," the mother whispered to the daughter.

"Yes, Mother, I feel so uncomfortable. What shall I *do?*"

"He's in love with you."

"In love with me? How can you tell?"

"Because I'm your mother."

"But what shall I do?"

"Nothing. He'll try to talk to you. If he does, answer him. Be nice to him. He's only a boy."

The train reached the business district and many people got off. The girl and her mother found seats opposite the young man. He continued to look at the girl who occasionally looked to see if he was looking at her.

The young man found a good pretext for standing in giving his seat to an elderly man.* He stood over the girl and her mother. They whispered back and forth and looked up at him. At another stop the seat next to the girl was vacated, and the young man blushed but quickly took it.

"I knew it," the mother said between her teeth. "I knew it, I knew it."

The young man cleared his throat and tapped the girl. She jumped.

"Pardon me," he said. "You're a very pretty girl."

"Thank you," she said.

"Don't talk to him," her mother said. "Don't answer him. I'm warning you. Believe me."

"I'm in love with you," he said to the girl.

"I don't believe you," the girl said.

"Don't answer him," the mother said.

"I really do," he said. "In fact, I'm so much in love with you that I want to marry you."

"Do you have a job?" she said.

* This sentence means: "The young man found a good reason to stand up by giving his seat to an elderly man."

"Yes, today is my first day. I'm going to Manhattan to start my first day of work."

"What kind of work will you do?" she asked.

"I don't know exactly," he said. "You see, I didn't start yet."

"It sounds exciting," she said.

"It's my first job, but I'll have my own desk and handle a lot of papers and carry them around in a briefcase, and it will pay well, and I'll work my way up."

"I love you," she said.

"Will you marry me?"

"I don't know. You'll have to ask my mother."

The young man rose from his seat and stood before the girl's mother. He cleared his throat very carefully for a long time. "May I have the honor of having your daughter's hand in marriage?" he said, but he was drowned out by the subway noise.

The mother looked up at him and said, "What?" He couldn't hear her either, but he could tell by the movement of her lips and by the way her face wrinkled up that she said, What.

The train pulled to a stop.

"May I have the honor of having your daughter's hand in marriage!" he shouted, not realizing there was no subway noise. Everybody on the train looked at him, smiled, and then they all applauded.

"Are you crazy?" the mother asked.

The train started again.

"What?" he said.

"Why do you want to marry her?" she asked.

"Well, she's pretty—I mean, I'm in love with her."

"Is that all?"

"I guess so," he said. "Is there supposed to be more?"

"No. Not usually," the mother said. "Are you working?"

"Yes. As a matter of fact, that's why I'm going into Manhattan so early. Today is the first day of my first job."

"Congratulations," the mother said.

"Thanks," he said. "Can I marry your daughter?"

"Do you have a car?" she asked.

"Not yet," he said. "But I should be able to get one pretty soon. And a house, too."

"A house?"

"With lots of rooms."

"Yes, that's what I expected you to say," she said. She turned to her daughter. "Do you love him?"

"Yes, Mother, I do."

"Why?"

"Because he's good, and gentle, and kind."

"Are you sure?"

"Yes."

"Then you really love him."

"Yes."

"Are you sure there isn't anyone else that you might love and might want to marry?"

"No, Mother," the girl said.

"Well, then," the mother said to the young man. "Looks like there's nothing I can do about it. Ask her again."

The train stopped.

"My dearest one," he said, "will you marry me?"

"Yes," she said.

Everybody in the car smiled and applauded.

"Isn't life wonderful?" the boy asked the mother.

"Beautiful," the mother said.

The conductor climbed down from between the cars as the train started up and, straightening his dark tie, approached them with a solemn black book in his hand.

Check Your Understanding

Put the events of the story back in order. Put a 1 by the event that happened first, a 2 by the event that happened second, and so forth. The first event has been done for you.

a. The young man tells the girl he is in love with her. ________

b. The young man stares at the girl. ________

c. The young man asks the girl to marry him. ________

d. The young man asks the girl a second time to marry him. ________

e. The mother asks the young man if he has a house. ________

f. The girl wants to know if the young man has a job and car. ________

g. The girl tells her mother she loves the young man. ________

h. The conductor approaches them with a black book in his hand. ________

i. Everyone on the train car claps for the young couple. ________

j. He sees a woman and her daughter on the subway train. ________

k. A young man takes the subway to his first day at a new job. ___1___

l. A seat becomes empty near the girl, and the young man takes it. ________

Group Discussion

Talk about these questions with your group or a partner.

1. Did you like this story? Why or why not?
2. What is a fable? What other fables do you know?
3. Why is the story called "A Fable"?

Language Focus: Two-Word Verbs

These two-word verbs are found in your reading. Complete each sentence with the correct verb. Change any words you need to make the sentences correct.

get on *get off* *drown out* *work [one's way] up* *start up*

Example: When you enter a bus you get on.

1. I couldn't hear at all. The sound of the train ______________ the music.
2. If you are interested in success, you will ______________.
3. Jerry ______________ the horse carefully when he finishes riding.
4. On cold days, I ______________ the car ten minutes before I leave for work.
5. To ride a bicycle, you must ______________ the seat and pedal.
6. She got in her car and ______________ the engine.
7. We tried to ______________ the baby's crying by singing.
8. When a plane lands, people ______________ very slowly.

Second Step

Vocabulary

These words are found in the reading. Check the ones you know. Write a short definition for each.

☐ *tenant:* ______________________________

____

☐ *linoleum:* ______________________________

____

☐ *unreprimanded:* ____________________

____

☐ *slits:* ____________________

____

☐ *lured:* ____________________

____

☐ *gazed:* ____________________

____

☐ *linen:* ____________________

____

☐ *platter:* ____________________

____

☐ *hoarsely:* ____________________

____

☐ *cutlery:* ____________________

____

☐ *brittle:* ____________________

____

☐ *canal:* ____________________

____

☐ *eroded:* ____________________

____

☐ *scorched:* ____________________

____

☐ *parched:* ______________________________

____

☐ *fervently:* ______________________________

____

☐ *wringing:* ______________________________

____

Reading

I See You Never

by Ray Bradbury

About the Author: Ray Bradbury is best known for writing science fiction. However, he has written many different types of stories during his long career. His most famous books include The Martian Chronicles *and* Fahrenheit 451. *Many of his stories have become movies or television shows. Bradbury has helped make science fiction a respected type of literature. He was born in 1920 in Illinois. He wrote for magazines before writing books. During his life, he has written 20 novels and dozens of short story collections. The following story, "I See You Never," was written in 1946.*

The soft knock came at the kitchen door, and when Mrs. O'Brian opened it, there on the back porch were her best tenant, Mr. Ramirez, and two police officers, one on each side of him. Mr. Ramirez just stood there, walled in and small.

"Why, Mr. Ramirez!" said Mrs. O'Brian.

Mr. Ramirez was overcome. He did not seem to have words to explain.

He had arrived at Mrs. O'Brian's rooming house more than two years earlier and had lived there ever since. He had come by bus from Mexico City to San Diego and had then gone up to Los Angeles. There he had found the clean little room, with glossy blue linoleum, and pictures and calendars on the flowered walls, and Mrs. O'Brian as the strict but kindly landlady. During the war, he had worked at the airplane factory and made parts for the planes that flew off somewhere, and even now, after the war, he still held his job. From the first, he had made big money. He saved some of it, and he got drunk only once a week—a privilege that, to Mrs. O'Brian's way of thinking, every good workingman deserved, unquestioned and unreprimanded.

Inside Mrs. O'Brian's kitchen, pies were baking in the oven. Soon the pies would come out with complexions like Mr. Ramirez's, brown and shiny and crisp, with slits in them for the air almost like the slits of Mr. Ramirez's dark eyes. The kitchen smelled good. The policemen leaned forward, lured by the odor. Mr. Ramirez gazed at his feet, as if they had carried him into all this trouble.

"What happened, Mr. Ramirez?" asked Mrs. O'Brian.

Behind Mrs. O'Brian, as he lifted his eyes, Mr. Ramirez saw the long table, laid with clean white linen and set with a platter, cool, shining glasses, a water pitcher with ice cubes floating inside it, a bowl of fresh potato salad, and one of bananas and oranges, cubed and sugared. At this table sat Mrs. O'Brian's children—her three grown sons, eating and conversing, and her two younger daughters, who were staring at the policemen as they ate.

"I have been here thirty months," said Mr. Ramirez quietly, looking at Mrs. O'Brian's plump hands.

"That's six months too long," said one policeman. "He only had a temporary visa. We've just got around to looking for him."

Soon after Mr. Ramirez had arrived, he bought a radio for his little room; evenings, he turned it up very loud and enjoyed it. And he had bought a wrist-watch and enjoyed that, too.

And on many nights he had walked silent streets and seen the bright clothes in the windows and bought some of them, and he had seen the jewels and bought some of them for his few lady friends. And he had gone to picture shows five nights a week for a while. Then, also, he had ridden the streetcars—all night some nights—smelling the electricity, his dark eyes moving over the advertisements, feeling the wheels rumble under him, watching the little sleeping houses and big hotels slip by. Besides that, he had gone to large restaurants, where he had eaten many-course dinners, and to the opera and the theatre. And he had bought a car, which later, when he forgot to pay for it, the dealer had driven off angrily from in front of the rooming house.

"So here I am," said Mr. Ramirez now, "to tell you that I must give up my room, Mrs. O'Brian. I come to get my baggage and clothes and go with these men."

"Back to Mexico?"

"Yes. To Lagos. That is a little town north of Mexico City."

"I'm sorry, Mr. Ramirez."

"I'm packed," said Mr. Ramirez hoarsely, blinking his dark eyes rapidly and moving his hands helplessly before him. The policemen did not touch him. There was no necessity for that. "Here is the key, Mrs. O'Brian," Mr. Ramirez said, "I have my bag already."

Mrs. O'Brian, for the first time, noticed a suitcase standing behind him on the porch.

Mr. Ramirez looked in again at the huge kitchen, at the bright silver cutlery and the young people eating and the shining waxed floor. He turned and looked for a long moment at the apartment house next door, rising up three stories, high and beautiful. He looked at the balconies and fire escapes and back-porch stairs, at the lines of laundry snapping in the wind.

"You've been a good tenant," said Mrs. O'Brian.

"Thank you, thank you, Mrs. O'Brian," he said softly. He closed his eyes.

Mrs. O'Brian stood holding the door half open. One of her sons, behind her, said that her dinner was getting cold, but she shook her head at him and turned back to Mr. Ramirez. She remembered a visit she had once made to some Mexican border towns—the hot days, the endless crickets leaping and falling or lying dead and brittle like the small cigars in the shop windows' and the canals taking river water out to the farms, the dirt roads, the scorched fields, the little adobe houses, the bleached clothes, the eroded landscape. She remembered the silent towns, the warm beer, the hot, thick foods each day. She remembered the slow, dragging horses and the parched jack rabbits on the road. She remembered the iron mountains and the dusty valleys and the ocean beaches that spread hundreds of miles with no sound but the waves—no cars, no buildings, nothing.

"I'm sure sorry, Mr. Ramirez," she said.

"I don't want to go back, Mrs. O'Brian," he said weakly. "I like it here. I want to stay here. I've worked, I've got money. I look all right, don't I? And I don't want to go back!"

"I'm sorry, Mr. Ramirez," she said. "I wish there was something I could do."

"Mrs. O'Brian!" he cried suddenly, tears rolling out from under his eyelids. He reached out his hands and took her hand fervently, shaking it, wringing it, holding to it. "Mrs. O'Brian, I see you never, I see you never!"

The policemen smiled at this, but Mr. Ramirez did not notice it, and they stopped smiling very soon.

"Goodbye, Mrs. O'Brian. You have been good to me. Oh, goodbye, Mrs. O'Brian. I see you never!"

The policemen waited for Mr. Ramirez to turn, pick up his suitcase, and walk away. Then they followed him, tipping their caps to Mrs. O'Brian. She watched them go down the porch steps. Then she shut the door quietly and went slowly back to her chair at the table. She pulled the chair out and sat down. She picked up the shining knife and fork and started once more upon her steak.

"Hurry up, Mom," said one of the sons. "It'll be cold."

Mrs. O'Brian took one bite and chewed on it for a long, slow time; then she stared at the closed door. She laid down her knife and fork.

"What's wrong, Ma?" asked her son.

"I just realized," said Mrs. O'Brian—she put her hand to her face—"I'll never see Mr. Ramirez again."

Check Your Understanding

Choose the correct answer. Check your answers with a partner or group.

1. What is the relationship between Mrs. O'Brian and Mr. Ramirez?
   a. Mr. Ramirez owns a house where Mrs. O'Brian lives.
   b. Mrs. O'Brian and Mr. Ramirez rent apartments in the same building.
   c. Mr. Ramirez rents a room in Mrs. O'Brian's house.
   d. Mr. Ramirez is Mrs. O'Brian's neighbor.
2. Why is Mr. Ramirez returning to Mexico?
   a. He wants to go home.
   b. He overstayed his U.S. visa.
   c. Mrs. O'Brian asked him to.
   d. He got drunk.
3. What is Mrs. O'Brian's memory of her visit to Mexico?
   a. She remembers it was hot, dusty, and dry.
   b. She remembers it was very beautiful.
   c. She remembers people smoked cigars.
   d. She remembers it was very noisy.
4. What word describes Mr. Ramirez's experience in the United States?
   a. difficult
   b. cold
   c. enjoyable
   d. angry
5. What kind of person is Mrs. O'Brian?
   a. beautiful but mean
   b. strict but kind
   c. clean and little
   d. cold and uncaring

Group Discussion

Talk about these questions with your group or a partner.

1. Does Mrs. O'Brian care about Mr. Ramirez? Explain your answer.
2. Compare Mr. Ramirez's memory of the United States and Mrs. O'Brian's memory of Mexico. Why are they so different?
3. Should Mrs. O'Brian have reacted differently? Explain your answer.
4. Did you enjoy this story? Why or why not?

Language Focus: Adjective Order

This story is very descriptive; it uses a lot of adjectives. In some cases, more than one adjective is used to describe something. For example:

> There he had found a *clean little* room, with *glossy blue* linoleum.

In English, adjectives usually appear in a specific order, as follows:

modifier	**size**	**color**	**material**	**NOUN**
shiny	big	green	metal	*vase*
very	tiny	brown	wooden	*box*

Here are nouns and adjectives found in the story. Write sentences in which you use the number of adjectives indicated in parentheses.

Adjectives					
clean	shining	flowered	good	white	silver
fresh	loud	bright	beautiful	very	slow
glossy	brown	crisp	long	cool	brittle
little	blue	shiny	dusty	dark	hot

Nouns					
room	wall	table	clothes	fork	car
calendar	odor	pitcher	jewels	laundry	bowl

1. (2) ______________________________

____

2. (2) ______________________________

____

3. (3) ______________________________

____

4. (3) ______________________________

____

5. (4) ______________________________

____

6. (4) ______________________________

____

Third Step

Vocabulary

These words are in the reading. Find them in an English-English dictionary. Discuss their definition with a classmate or your teacher. Write the meanings, and in your own words, write a sample sentence that shows you understand the meaning. (See page 12 for an example.)

1. *magnificence:* ______________________________

____

Sample sentence: ______________________________

____

2. *longing:* ____

____

Sample sentence: ____

____

3. *pious:* ____

____

Sample sentence: ____

____

4. *capricious:* ____

____

Sample sentence: ____

____

5. *alfalfa:* ____

____

Sample sentence: ____

____

6. *hearty:* ____

____

Sample sentence: ____

____

7. *surrey:* ____

____

Sample sentence: ____

____

Reading

Reading Note: *The San Joaquin Valley is a farming area in central California.*

The Summer of the Beautiful White Horse

excerpt from *My Name Is Aram*
by William Saroyan

About the Author: William Saroyan was born in Fresno, California, in 1908. He wrote novels, short stories, plays, and essays. He was a high-school dropout who was self-educated. When he was young, he decided to become a writer. He wrote about his experience as an Armenian-American growing up in California. His first published story appeared in The Overland Monthly *in 1928. He died in Fresno on May 18, 1981.*

One day back there in the good old days when I was nine and the world was full of every imaginable kind of magnificence, and life was still a delightful and mysterious dream, my cousin Mourad, who was considered crazy by everybody who knew him except me, came to my house at four in the morning and woke me up by tapping on the window of my room.

Aram, he said.

I jumped out of bed and looked out the window.

I couldn't believe what I saw.

It wasn't morning yet, but it was summer and with daybreak not many minutes around the corner of the world it was light enough for me to know I wasn't dreaming.

My cousin Mourad was sitting on a beautiful white horse.

I stuck my head out of the window and rubbed my eyes.

Yes, he said in Armenian. It's a horse. You're not dreaming. Make it quick if you want a ride.

I knew my cousin Mourad enjoyed being alive more than anybody else who had ever fallen into the world by mistake, but this was more than even I could believe.

In the first place, my earliest memories had been memories of horses and my first longings had been longings to ride.

This was the wonderful part.

In the second place, we were poor.

This was the part that wouldn't permit me to believe what I saw.

We were poor. We had no money. Our whole tribe was poverty-stricken. Every branch of the Garoghlanian family was living in the most amazing and comical poverty in the world. Nobody could understand where we ever got money enough to keep us with food in our bellies, not even the old men of the family. Most important of all, though, we were famous for our honesty. We had been famous for our honesty for something like eleven centuries, even when we had been the wealthiest family in what we liked to think was the world. We were proud first, honest next, and after that we believed in right and wrong. None of us would take advantage of anybody in the world, let alone steal.

Consequently, even though I could see the horse, so magnificent; even though I could *smell* it, so lovely; even though I could *hear* it breathing, so exciting; I couldn't *believe* the horse had anything to do with my cousin Mourad or with me or with any of the other members of our family, asleep or awake, because I *knew* my cousin Mourad couldn't have *bought* the horse, and if he couldn't have bought it he must have *stolen* it, and I refused to believe he had stolen it.

No member of the Garoghlanian family could be a thief.

I stared first at my cousin and then at the horse. There was a pious stillness and humor in each of them which on the one hand delighted me and on the other frightened me.

Mourad, I said, where did you steal this horse?

Leap out of the window, he said, if you want a ride.

It was true, then. He *had* stolen the horse. There was no question about it. He had come to invite me to ride or not, as I chose.

Well, it seemed to me stealing a horse for a ride was not the same thing as stealing something else, such as money. For all I knew, maybe it wasn't stealing at all. If you were crazy about horses the way my cousin Mourad and I were, it wasn't stealing. It wouldn't become stealing until we offered to sell the horse, which of course I knew we would never do.

Let me put on some clothes, I said.

All right, he said, but hurry.

I leaped into my clothes.

I jumped down to the yard from the window and leaped up onto the horse behind my cousin Mourad.

That year we lived at the edge of town, on Walnut Avenue. Behind our house was the country: vineyards, orchards, irrigation ditches, and country roads. In less than three minutes we were on Olive Avenue, and then the horse began to trot. The air was new and lovely to breathe. The feel of the horse running was wonderful. My cousin Mourad who was considered one of the craziest members of our family began to sing. I mean, he began to roar.

Every family has a crazy streak in it somewhere, and my cousin Mourad was considered the natural descendant of the crazy streak in our tribe. Before him was our uncle Khosrove, an enormous man with a powerful head of black hair and the largest mustache in the San Joaquin Valley, a man so furious in temper, so irritable, so impatient that he stopped anyone from talking by roaring, *It is no harm; pay no attention to it.*

That was all, no matter what anybody happened to be talking about. Once it was his own son Arak running eight blocks to the barber shop where his father was having his mustache trimmed to tell him their house was on fire. The man Khosrove sat up in the chair and roared, It is no harm; pay no attention to it. The barber said, But the boy says your house is on fire. So Khosrove roared, Enough, it is no harm, I say.

My cousin Mourad was considered the natural descendant of this man, although Mourad's father was Zorab, who was practical and nothing else. That's how it was in our tribe. A man could be the father of his son's flesh, but that did not mean that he was also the father of his spirit. The distribution of the various kinds of spirit of our tribe had been from the beginning capricious and vagrant.

We rode and my cousin Mourad sang. For all anybody knew we were still in the old country where, at least according to our neighbors, we belonged. We let the horse run as long as it felt like running.

At last my cousin Mourad said, Get down. I want to ride alone.

Will you let me ride alone? I said.

That is up to the horse, my cousin said. Get down.

The *horse* will let me ride, I said.

We shall see, he said. Don't forget that I have a way with a horse.

Well, I said, any way you have with a horse, I have also.

For the sake of your safety, he said, let us hope so. Get down.

All right, I said, but remember you've got to let me try to ride alone.

I got down and my cousin Mourad kicked his heels into the horse and shouted, *Vazire*, run. The horse stood on its hind legs, snorted, and burst into a fury of speed that was the loveliest thing I had ever seen. My cousin Mourad raced the horse across a field of dry grass to an irrigation ditch, crossed the ditch on the horse, and five minutes later returned, dripping wet.

The sun was coming up.

Now it's my turn to ride, I said.

My cousin Mourad got off the horse.

Ride, he said.

I leaped to the back of the horse and for a moment knew the awfulest fear imaginable. The horse did not move.

Kick into his muscles, my cousin Mourad said. What are you waiting for? We've got to take him back before everybody in the world is up and about.

I kicked into the muscles of the horse. Once again it reared and snorted. Then it began to run. I didn't know what to do. Instead of running across the field to the irrigation ditch the horse ran down the road to the vineyard of Dikran Halabian where it began to leap over vines. The horse leaped over seven vines before I fell. Then it continued running.

My cousin Mourad came running down the road.

I'm not worried about you, he shouted. We've got to get that horse. You go this way and I'll go this way. If you come upon him, be kindly. I'll be near.

I continued down the road and my cousin Mourad went across the field toward the irrigation ditch.

It took him half an hour to find the horse and bring him back.

All right, he said, jump on. The whole world is awake now.

What will we do? I said.

Well, he said, we'll either take him back or hide him until tomorrow morning.

He didn't sound worried and I knew he'd hide him and not take him back. Not for a while, at any rate.

Where will you hide him? I said.

I know a place, he said.

How long ago did you steal this horse? I said.

It suddenly dawned on me that he had been taking these early morning rides for some time and had come for me this morning only because he knew how much I longed to ride.

Who said anything about stealing a horse? he said.

Anyhow, I said, how long ago did you begin riding every morning?

Not until this morning, he said.

Are you telling the truth? I said.

Of course not, he said, but if we are found out, that's what you're to say. I don't want both of us to be liars. All you know is that we started riding this morning.

All right, I said.

He walked the horse quietly to the barn of a deserted vineyard which at one time had been the pride of a farmer named Fetvajian. There were some oats and dry alfalfa in the barn.

We began walking home.

It wasn't easy, he said, to get the horse to behave so nicely. At first it wanted to run wild, but as I've told you, I have a way with a horse. I can get it to want to do anything I want it to do. Horses understand me.

How do you do it? I said.

I have an understanding with a horse, he said.

Yes, but what sort of an understanding? I said.

A simple and honest one, he said.

Well, I said, I wish I knew how to reach an understanding like that with a horse.

You're still a small boy, he said. When you get to be thirteen you'll know how to do it.

I went home and ate a hearty breakfast.

That afternoon my uncle Khosrove came to our house for coffee and cigarettes. He sat in the parlor, sipping and smoking and remembering the old country. Then another visitor arrived, a farmer named John Byro, an Assyrian who, out of loneliness, had learned to speak Armenian. My mother brought the lonely visitor coffee and tobacco and he rolled a cigarette and sipped and smoked, and then at last, sighing sadly, he said, My white horse which was stolen last month is still gone. I cannot understand it.

My uncle Khosrove became very irritated and shouted, It's no harm. What is the loss of a horse? Haven't we all lost the homeland? What is this crying over a horse?

That may be all right for you, a city dweller, to say, John Byro said, but what of my surrey? What good is a surrey without a horse?

Pay no attention to it, my uncle Khosrove roared.

I walked ten miles to get here, John Byro said.

You have legs, my uncle Khosrove shouted.

My left leg pains me, the farmer said.

Pay no attention to it, my uncle Khosrove roared.

That horse cost me sixty dollars, the farmer said.

I spit on money, my uncle Khosrove said.

He got up and stalked out of the house, slamming the screen door.

My mother explained.

He has a gentle heart, she said. It is simply that he is homesick and such a large man.

The farmer went away and I ran over to my cousin Mourad's house.

He was sitting under a peach tree, trying to repair the hurt wing of a young robin which could not fly. He was talking to the bird.

What is it? he said.

The farmer, John Byro, I said. He visited our house. He wants his horse. You've had it a month. I want you to promise not to take it back until I learn to ride.

It will take you a *year* to learn to ride, my cousin Mourad said.

We could keep the horse a year, I said.

My cousin Mourad leaped to his feet.

What? he roared. Are you inviting a member of the Garoghlanian family to steal? The horse must go back to its true owner.

When? I said.

In six months at the latest, he said.

He threw the bird into the air. The bird tried hard, almost fell twice, but at last flew away, high and straight.

Early every morning for two weeks my cousin Mourad and I took the horse out of the barn of the deserted vineyard where we were hiding it and rode it, and every morning the horse, when it was my turn to ride alone, leaped over grape vines and small trees and threw me and ran away. Nevertheless, I hoped in time to learn to ride the way my cousin Mourad rode.

One morning on the way to Fetvajian's deserted vineyard we ran into the farmer John Byro who was on his way to town.

Let me do the talking, my cousin Mourad said. I have a way with farmers.

Good morning, John Byro, my cousin Mourad said to the farmer.

The farmer studied the horse eagerly.

Good morning, sons of my friends, he said. What is the name of your horse?

My Heart, my cousin Mourad said in Armenian.

A lovely name, John Byro said, for a lovely horse. I could swear it is the horse that was stolen from me many weeks ago. May I look into its mouth?

Of course, Mourad said.

The farmer looked into the mouth of the horse.

Tooth for tooth, he said. I would swear it *is* my horse if I didn't know your parents. The fame of your family for honesty is well known to me. Yet the horse is the twin of my horse. A suspicious man would believe his eyes instead of his heart. Good day, my young friends.

Good day, John Byro, my cousin Mourad said.

Early the following morning we took the horse to John Byro's vineyard and put it in the barn. The dogs followed us around without making a sound.

The dogs, I whispered to my cousin Mourad. I thought they would bark.

They would at somebody else, he said. I have a way with dogs.

My cousin Mourad put his arms around the horse, pressed his nose into the horse's nose, patted it, and then we went away.

That afternoon John Byro came to our house in his surrey and showed my mother the horse that had been stolen and returned.

I do not know what to think, he said. The horse is stronger than ever. Better-tempered, too. I thank God.

My uncle Khosrove, who was in the parlor, became irritated and shouted, Quiet, man, quiet. Your horse has been returned. Pay no attention to it.

Check Your Understanding

Complete each sentence with the correct answer from the story.

1. The main character and narrator's name is ____________________.
2. The main character's cousin is named ____________________.
3. The farmer's name is ____________________.
4. This story takes place in ____________________ of California.
5. The characters speak a language called ____________________.
6. ____________________ always says, "It is no harm; pay no attention to it."
7. Mourad's father's name is ____________________.
8. The main character is ____________________ years old.
9. The Garoghlanian family was famous for its ____________________.
10. Mourad steals a horse named ____________________.

Group Discussion

Talk about these questions with your group or a partner.

1. What kind of person is Aram? Find a passage in the story that demonstrates this.
2. What kind of person is Mourad? Find a passage in the story that demonstrates this.
3. Why did the boys return the horse, in your opinion?
4. Why did Uncle Khosrove become irritated with the farmer after the horse was returned?
5. What did you learn about life for Armenians in California's central valley?
6. Did you enjoy this story? Why or why not?

Language Focus: Idioms

Fill in the blanks with the correct idiom from the list. Change any words you need to in order to make the sentences grammatical.

let alone	*on the one hand*
no question about it	*crazy about*
no matter what	*for all anybody knew*
for the sake of	~~*dawn on*~~
has a way with	*the old country*

1. It ___dawned on___ Aram that Mourad had been taking these early morning rides for nearly a month.
2. ________________, they were still in the old country where they belonged.
3. Mourad had stolen the horse—there was ________________.
4. ________________ his safety, Aram got down from the horse.
5. Mourad was good with animals. He ________________ a horse.
6. None of them would take advantage of anybody, ________________ steal.
7. Mourad and Aram were ________________ horses—they loved them so much.
8. Uncle Khosrove sat in the parlor, remembering ________________ and his boyhood.
9. It was true, ________________ anybody thought. Mourad stole the horse.
10. ________________ Aram was delighted with the horse, and on the other, he was afraid they would be caught stealing.

Chapter Wrap-Up

Speaking Activities

Class Reports

1. Meet with students who read the same reading you did. Review the questions at the end of the reading.
2. Think of one question to ask your group about the reading. Take turns asking your questions.
3. Choose someone from your group to give a report to the class. In your report, tell your classmates what you learned from your reading.
4. Choose one part of the story you like. Write it out as a dialogue. Perform your dialogue for the class.
5. Teach students in other groups one important word you learned from this chapter.

Discussion

1. Do you enjoy reading stories? Why or why not?
2. Have you heard of any of the writers in this chapter, Ray Bradbury, William Saroyan, or Robert Fox? What do you know about them?
3. Do you prefer movies to reading? Why or why not?
4. What is your favorite book or movie?

Writing Ideas

Look at the cartoon drawing on page 68. What is this story? Write the story in your own words.

Write a summary of *I See You Never* in not more than 150 words. Compare your summary with a partner's. What details did you include? What did you leave out? Rewrite your summary to improve it.

Do you think John Byro knew the boys had stolen his horse? Write two to three paragraphs stating your opinion. Support your opinion with quotations from the story.

Choose a sentence or passage from the story that you found difficult to understand. Rewrite it in your own words, and explain what it means.

For Your Journal

Write about a place from your childhood. Describe what it looked like. Tell a story that happened there.

CHAPTER

5 Art

Art of the Americas

Icebreaker

The Aztec Calendar

Discuss these questions with a partner or a group. Write down the answers.

1. Do you like to draw or paint?
2. Do you have a favorite artist?
3. Do you like to visit museums?
4. What kind of art do you like best?

CHAPTER PREVIEW

What things do you know about art in the Americas? Answer these questions to find out:

1. Do you know where the Northwest Territories are? *yes* *no*
2. Have you heard of the Nasca Lines of Peru? *yes* *no*
3. Have you read anything or seen movies about Frida Kahlo and Diego Rivera? *yes* *no*

Explain your answer: ______________________________

____

____

____

This chapter presents art from different areas and people of the Americas: Canada, Peru, and Mexico.

First Step

Vocabulary

These words are in your reading. Fill in the blanks with the correct choice.

a. *inland*	e. *thigh*	i. *hazy*
b. *caribou*	f. *walrus*	j. *transport*
c. *secure*	g. *hatch*	k. *bearded*
d. *refresh*	h. *indication*	

Example: This large animal has big teeth. It lives in the water. It is called a walrus.

1. Another way of saying *to get* something is to ______________ it.
2. If you are tired, you want to ______________ yourself.

3. If you have an *idea* or a *clue* that something will happen, you have an ________________ of it.
4. It might be difficult to see when it is ________________ outdoors.
5. The area in the middle of the country is ________________ from the shore.
6. The top part of your leg is called your ________________.
7. This animal is like a deer. It is called a ________________.
8. To take something from one place to another is to ________________ it.
9. When birds come out of their eggs, they ________________.
10. If someone has facial hair, he might be ________________.

Reading

> **Reading Note:** *This reading is an interview. One person is asking questions to two others, whose initials are EN and TI.*

Trip Inland in Summer

About the Author: EN and TI live in Cape Dorset, located in far northern Canada. They are members of the Igloolik, who are a group of First Nations people of the Northwest Territories. They are discussing the meaning of the drawing on page 100.

EN: We use* to walk all the way inland to spend the summer.

TI: Ever since I was a child, I use to walk all around.

EN: The reason was that there were no caribou close by at that time. That was the only way we use to hunt caribou so that we could secure the skin for clothing.

* The correct grammar is "I used to walk"; however, many people say and write "use to walk."

TI: On the first day that you started out you would walk all day long, when night came you would set up camp. One felt so tired. After we woke up the following morning we would be refreshed again, as if we had never been tired.

EN: The first day your thighs would be really sore, then the second day you would not get as tired, then the third day you would no longer get tired.

Q. *So you would stay in this area in the spring and when the summer arrived then you would go inland for the summer?*

EN: In the summer the men would be hunting for walrus while there was daylight all of the time.

TI: When small birds had hatched and started to walk around, that was an indication that it was time for you to go inland. That was the time when you went inland for the summer.

EN: That is also the time when it started to get hazy at night. At the same time there would be those that would start to move to the places where they would be spending the summer. As for ourselves, we would be transported by boat to the place where we would start inland.

TI: In our case we would be taken to the mainland while the ice was still solid. We would be on the littoral* hunting for bearded seal before the summer.

Check Your Understanding

Choose the correct answer.

1. Why did EN and TI walk inland in the summer?
   a. They liked to walk all around.
   b. There were no caribou near.
   c. It was more refreshing there.
2. Why did EN and TI hunt caribou?
   a. They had to get food for the winter.
   b. They used them when they set up camp.
   c. They used their skin for clothing.
3. Why did EN's and TI's thighs get sore?
   a. from walking
   b. from hunting
   c. from setting up camp
4. When did the men hunt for walrus?
   a. in the spring
   b. in the winter
   c. in the summer

* A "littoral" is a seashore or the area near it.

5. What was the sign that it was time to go inland?
   a. the caribou came
   b. the birds hatched
   c. the walrus went away

6. Where were EN and TI before summer?
   a. on the coast, hunting seal
   b. on the mainland, hunting caribou
   c. inland, hatching birds

Group Discussion

Talk about these questions with your group or a partner.

1. Look at the picture on page 100. Describe to your group what is happening in the picture.
2. Do you like to walk places? Have you ever walked a long distance?
3. Have your parents told you stories about their childhoods? What have they told you? What seems surprising or old-fashioned today?

Language Focus: Animal Names

This reading presents some names of animals found in northern Canada. Describe the animals that are listed. Then, think of six more animal names, and describe them.

1. *walrus:* This large animal has big teeth. It lives in the water. It looks black and has large whiskers on its face.
2. *caribou:* ____________________
3. *seal:* ____________________

4. *bird:* ______________________________

____

5. ______________: ______________________________

____

6. ______________: ______________________________

____

7. ______________: ______________________________

____

8. ______________: ______________________________

____

9. ______________: ______________________________

____

10. ______________: ______________________________

____

Second Step

Vocabulary

These words are in the reading. Find them in an English-English dictionary. Discuss their definition with a classmate or your teacher. Write the meanings, and write a sample sentence in your own words that shows you understand the meaning. (See page 12 for an example.)

1. *parallel:* ______________________________

____

Sample sentence: ______________________________

____

2. *trapezoid:* ______________________________

____

Sample sentence: ______________________________

____

3. *crisscross:* ______________________________

____

Sample sentence: ______________________________

____

4. *gravel:* ______________________________

____

Sample sentence: ______________________________

____

5. *tarmac:* ______________________________

____

Sample sentence: ______________________________

____

6. *observatory:* ______________________________

____

Sample sentence: ______________________________

____

7. *shrine:* ______________________________

____

Sample sentence: ______________________________

____

8. *aqueduct:* ______________________________

____

Sample sentence: ______________________________

____

Reading

The Mystery of Nasca

There is a flat plain in the Peruvian desert between the Inca and Nasca Valleys, south of Lima. This area is 1 mile wide and 37 miles long, and contains a collection of straight lines, both parallel and intersecting, which form a huge geometric shape. In and around these lines there are also trapezoidal zones, strange symbols, and pictures of different birds and beasts.

There are two kinds of figures in the valley: *biomorphs* and *geoglyphs*. Biomorphs are animal and plant figures including a monkey, a spider, a hummingbird, and a 1,000-foot-long pelican. There are 70 biomorphs in the valley, which are grouped together. Some archaeologists think they were built around 200 BCE, around 500 years before the geoglyphs were made. Geoglyphs are geometric shapes, such as long straight lines and huge spirals, circles, triangles, and trapezoids. The longest straight line stretches for nine miles. There are about 900 geoglyphs.

What's surprising about these drawings is that you can't recognize them standing on Earth. They are all so large that they can only be recognized from the sky. As a result, they were not discovered in modern times until the 1930s, when an airplane pilot spotted them from above.

The pilot saw an area crisscrossed by these giant lines and rectangles. These lines were created by moving darkened stones to either side to expose the light-colored sand underneath. In fact, some people believe that the Nasca lines look like an airport. A Swiss writer, Erich von Daniken, even thought the lines had been created so that visitors from outer space could land their spaceships. However, the desert floor at Nasca is made up of soft soil and loose gravel; it is not hard like an airport tarmac. It certainly would not support the weight of an aircraft or a flying saucer.

An American explorer, Paul Kosok, who visited Nasca in the 1940s, had a different idea. He thought that the lines were astronomically significant—that the plain was like a huge space observatory. An American astronomer named Gerald Hawkins tested Kosok's theory in 1968. Hawkins put the positions of many of the lines into a computer, which then showed how many lines matched up with important astronomical events. Hawkins' results showed that it was unlikely that the Nasca lines were used as an observatory.

An English explorer, Tony Morrison, had an interesting theory about the lines, too. By researching the folkways* of the Andean people, Morrison discovered a tradition of shrines connected with straight paths. The worshipers walked from shrine to shrine, praying and meditating. Morrison believed that the Nasca lines had a similar purpose, but on a huge scale. The symbols may have marked out special areas for religious ceremonies. Johan Reinhard, another anthropologist, reports that modern villagers in Bolivia walk along a straight path to visit shrines while they pray and dance for rain. Reinhard believes something similar may have been done at the ancient Nasca lines.

Finally, two modern researchers, David Johnson and Steve Mabee, have yet another theory. They believe that the geoglyphs may be related to water. The Nasca plain is one of the driest places on Earth, with less than one inch of rain a year. Johnson was looking for sources of water in the area, and noticed that the Nasca lines connected some ancient aqueducts, called *puquios*. Johnson and Mabee believe that the shapes on the Nasca plain may make up a large map of underground water sources.

* "Folkways" are the cultural traditions and activities of a group of people.

> There are many theories about the Nasca lines. It is unclear whether their true use will ever be discovered. In the meantime, they spark the imagination of many researchers and visitors every day.

Check Your Understanding

Write a short answer to each of the questions. Check your answers with a partner or with your group.

1. In which country are the Nasca lines found? ______________
2. What are the two types of shapes found in the Nasca plain?

   ______________ and ______________
3. Which type of shape is older? ______________
4. How were the Nasca lines discovered? ______________________

   ____
5. What purpose did the writer Erich von Daniken believe the lines had?

   ____

   ____
6. What was Paul Kosok's theory? ______________________

   ____

   ____
7. According to Tony Morrison, what things do the lines connect together?

   ____

   ____

8. What do Johnson and Mabee think the lines were used for?

____

____

9. Why is it possible to see the Nasca lines only from the air?

____

____

Group Discussion

Talk about these questions with your group or a partner.

1. Which theory about the Nasca lines is most interesting, in your opinion?
2. Is it important to solve these ancient mysteries? Why or why not?
3. What is the most interesting or mysterious place you have visited?

Language Focus: Names of Shapes

This reading has many names for shapes of things. A good way to remember these kinds of words is to draw them. Draw an example of each of the shapes named, taken from the reading.

1. parallel lines	
2. intersecting lines	
3. trapezoid	
4. spiral	
5. triangle	

Third Step

Vocabulary

These words are found in the reading. Check the ones you know. Write a short definition for each.

- ☐ *leftist:* ______________________________
____
- ☐ *oust:* ______________________________
____
- ☐ *oblige:* ______________________________
____
- ☐ *convalescence:* ______________________________
____
- ☐ *surrealist:* ______________________________
____
- ☐ *beholder:* ______________________________
____
- ☐ *shaft:* ______________________________
____
- ☐ *exemplification:* ______________________________
____
- ☐ *mural:* ______________________________
____

☐ *fresco:* ____________________

____

☐ *caricature:* ____________________

____

☐ *depiction:* ____________________

____

☐ *defunct:* ____________________

____

☐ *intransigent:* ____________________

____

☐ *tableau:* ____________________

____

☐ *balk:* ____________________

____

☐ *emancipation:* ____________________

____

☐ *scaffold:* ____________________

____

☐ *furor:* ____________________

____

☐ *proletariat:* ____________________

____

☐ *marquee:* ______________________________

____

☐ *marquis:* ______________________________

____

☐ *anarchists:* ______________________________

____

☐ *lie in state:* ______________________________

____

☐ *wreath:* ______________________________

____

Reading: Frida and Diego

Reading Note: *The following two articles were obituaries, a short biography written upon someone's death.*

Frida Kahlo, Artist, Diego Rivera's Wife

From the *New York Times,* 1954

MEXICO CITY, July 13 (AP) Frida Kahlo, wife of Diego Rivera, the noted painter was found dead in her home today. Her age was 44. She had been suffering from cancer for several years.

She also was a painter and also had been active in leftist causes. She made her last public appearance in a wheelchair at a meeting here in support of the now ousted regime of Communist-backed President Jacobo Arbenz Guzman of Guatemala.

Frida Kahlo began painting in 1926 while obliged to lie in bed during convalescence from injuries suffered in a bus accident. Not long afterward she showed her work to Diego Rivera, who advised, "go on painting." They were married in 1929, began living apart in 1939, and were reunited in 1941.

Usually classed as a surrealist, the artist had no special explanation for her methods. She said only: "I put on the canvas whatever comes into my mind." She gave one-woman shows in Mexico City, New York and elsewhere, and is said to have been the first woman to sell a picture to the Louvre.*

Some of her pictures shocked beholders. One showed her with her hands cut off, a huge bleeding heart on the ground nearby, and on either side of her an empty dress. This was supposed to reveal how she felt when her husband went off alone on a trip. Another self-portrait presented the artist as a wounded deer, still carrying the shafts of nine arrows.

A year ago, too weak to stand for more than ten minutes, she sat daily at her easel, declaring: "I am happy to be alive as long as I can paint."

Diego Rivera Dies in Mexico at 70

From the *New York Times,* 1957

Painter, Controversial in His Art and Politics, Long Ill

MEXICO CITY, Nov. 25 (AP)—Diego Rivera, world-famed Mexican artist, died early this morning in his home here. He was 70 years old.

Señor Rivera had suffered from diabetes in the Nineteen Forties. Two years ago word leaked out that he had cancer and he went to Moscow for treatment by Soviet doctors. Early in 1956 he announced he had been cured by cobalt treatments and returned to Mexico City.

*The Louvre is a famous museum in Paris, France.

Señor Rivera, controversial in both art and politics, was once expelled from the Communist party and then readmitted on his own request.

He had been active until the last days of his recent illness.

Only his physician and members of his family were with him when he died at 1:15 A.M. [2:15 A.M., Eastern Standard Time.]

Uncompromisingly radical in word and work, head over heels in controversy his whole lifetime (at least from the age of 5, according to one story), Diego Rivera was the exemplification of an artistic renaissance in his native Mexico. He was this generation's best-known mural painter and the center of one of the most extraordinary episodes in the history of American art.

Physically huge, sweeping in thought and conception, Señor Rivera practiced in art's biggest hall, crowding into expanses of blank wall frescoes that championed the world's workers and cruelly caricatured persons of authority and wealth. As bitterly as he was assailed for his beliefs he was defended by many prominent artists and critics who had adjudged his massive depictions the work of a born master of the mural form. They placed him in the very forefront of the generation's creative activity.

His work sprawls across public walls in Mexico City, Los Angeles, Detroit and other cities. He has been represented in New York in the now defunct New Workers School. That series of thirteen panels, depicting the history of America is on permanent exhibition at Unity House, a vacation resort of the International Ladies Garment Workers Union, A.F.L.,* in Forest Park, Fla.

What might have become his most gazed upon work, a mural in the main building of Rockefeller Center, was carted away as dust and small chunks of plaster after the intransigent painter decided to make Nikolai Lenin the key figure of an enormous tableau, representing him as mankind's leader.

Rivera, who had gained his fame as a painter of Mexico's revolution, had been retained by the Rockefellers in 1933 and had submitted a preliminary sketch of his projected work, which had been approved. As his work progressed Nelson Rockefeller notified him that he thought the prominent place the portrait of Lenin had assumed "might easily offend a great many people."

* AFL is the American Federation of Labor, an organization of labor unions.

Got Fee for Unfinished Work

The artist was asked to substitute some unknown face. Rivera balked, arguing that such an alteration would destroy his conception of the fresco, which was to show the emancipation of mankind through technology. Halted while at work on the scaffold before the fresco the painter received $14,000, completing the payment of $21,000, his full fee for the commission, and the mural was covered with paper.

In the ensuing furor Señor Rivera charged that his work was being "assassinated," that "commercially minded people" had tampered with an issue of human rights that he described as "the right to create and the right to express truths as I see truths." He told Leftist sympathizers who rallied to his defense that he painted in the United States not merely as an artist but also to further the cause of the proletariat.

The Rockefeller Center incident was bizarre in many respects. Some pointed out that the Rockefellers could have had no illusions about Rivera's political doctrines when they retained him. Although he had been expelled from the Communist party in 1929 in Mexico his beliefs had undergone no real change.

In recent years, Rivera painted himself into fresh controversies.

In 1953, Roman Catholic organizations threatened a boycott of a new Mexico City theatre if Rivera painted the Virgin of Guadalupe in a huge outdoor mural over the marquee. There were protests that his portrayal of Mexico's patron saint was an "insult to the religion of the Mexican people." Rivera finally painted out the Virgin.

Son of Leading Citizen

Rivera was not a member of the proletariat but the son of a mine owner and one of the leading citizens of Guanajuato, Mexico. His full name was Diego Maria Concepcion Juan Nepomuceno Estanislao de la Rivera y Barrientos Acosta y Rodriguez. One of his ancestors was a Spanish marquis and a general.

His early painting won him a small scholarship for study abroad and brought him into contact not just with French and Spanish artists but also with the anarchists of Madrid.

At the first comprehensive show of his paintings and fresco details in this country, exhibited at the Museum of Modern Art in 1931,

Rivera was critically acclaimed, particularly for his interpretations of Mexican civilization and his depiction of the Indians.

The painter married four times, remarrying his third wife—Frida Kahlo, leftist, surrealist artist—after they had been separated. Miss Kahlo died in July, 1954, at the age of 44, and her death led to one of the last controversies in Rivera's life. It began when Miss Kahlo's coffin was draped in the Soviet Union flag while lying in state in the National Institute of Fine Arts in Mexico City.

There was an outcry for the dismissal of the institute's director, Dr. Andres Iduarte, and he lost his job. It was rumored that communists brought the coffin to the institute under a blanket of flower wreaths that hid the flag. Rivera, rebuked by Dr. Iduarte, threatened to take the coffin into the street for funeral services. Rather than permit this scene, it was said, Dr. Iduarte allowed the services to continue.

Check Your Understanding

Write *R* after each fact that is true for Diego Rivera, *K* for each that is true for Frida Kahlo, and *B* if it is true of both. If it is true of neither, leave it blank. Check your answers with a classmate's or with your group's.

1. Was a "leftist." ________
2. Suffered from cancer. ________
3. Was a surrealist. ________
4. Was a muralist. ________
5. Had a controversial funeral. ________
6. Was in a bus accident. ________
7. Suffered from diabetes. ________
8. Was hired to paint a project for the Rockefellers. ________
9. Was the child of a miner. ________
10. Painted frescoes. ________

11. Was surrounded by controversy. ________
12. Was assassinated. ________
13. Died at age 70. ________
14. Died at age 44. ________
15. Was buried in the United States. ________

Group Discussion

Talk about these questions with your group or a partner.

1. What is your opinion of the obituaries presented here? Do you think they would be written differently if they were written today?
2. Have you seen any other Kahlo or Rivera paintings (or photographs of them)? What do you remember about them?
3. Why was communism mentioned so frequently in the articles? How were times different then?

Language Focus: Understanding Complex Language

Reread the following sentences, and then rewrite them in your own words. Pay attention especially to the underlined parts of the sentences.

1. She made her last public appearance in a wheelchair at a meeting here [New York] <u>in support of the now ousted regime of Communist-backed</u> President Jacobo Arbenz Guzman of Guatemala.

 ____

 ____

 ____

2. Frida Kahlo began painting in 1926 while obliged to lie in bed during convalescence from injuries suffered in a bus accident.

3. Uncompromisingly radical in word and work, head over heels in controversy his whole lifetime (at least from the age of 5, according to one story), Diego Rivera was the exemplification of an artistic renaissance in his native Mexico.

4. Physically huge, sweeping in thought and conception, Señor Rivera practiced in art's biggest hall, crowding into expanses of blank wall frescoes that championed the world's workers and cruelly caricatured persons of authority and wealth.

5. As bitterly as he was assailed for his beliefs he was defended by many prominent artists and critics who had adjudged his massive depictions the work of a born master of the mural form.

6. What might have become his most gazed upon work, a mural in the main building of Rockefeller Center, was carted away as dust and small chunks of plaster after the intransigent painter decided to make Nikolai Lenin the key figure of an enormous tableau, representing him as mankind's leader.

7. He told Leftist sympathizers who rallied to his defense that he painted in the United States not merely as an artist but also to further the cause of the proletariat.

8. It began when Miss Kahlo's coffin was draped in the Soviet Union flag while lying in state in the National Institute of Fine Arts in Mexico City.

Chapter Wrap-Up

Speaking Activities

Class Reports

1. Meet with students who read the same reading you did. Review the questions at the end of the reading.
2. Think of one question to ask your group about the reading. Take turns asking your questions.

3. Choose someone from your group to give a report to the class. In your report, tell your classmates what you learned from your reading.

4. Show your classmates one or more of the pictures included with your reading. Explain the image to them.

Discussion

1. What was the most interesting part of your reading? Explain your answer.

2. Have you taken an art class? What was it like?

3. Do you like paintings or sculpture better? Why?

Writing Ideas

Choose one of the pictures in this chapter. Describe it. Explain why you like it.

Write a short explanation of the Nasca lines. Explain why someone would find them interesting.

Visit a museum, or find a book with artwork you like. Find a piece of artwork, and write a short description of it. Then, explain in two to three paragraphs why you like it.

Choose one of these artists:

Vincent van Gogh (The Netherlands)
Max Ernst (Germany/France)
Georgia O'Keeffe (United States)
Roberto Matta (Chile)
Marc Chagall (Russia/France)
Michelangelo (France)

On the Internet or in the library find information about the artist you chose. Write three or four paragraphs describing the artist's life. Use your own words.

For Your Journal

Is art important to you? Why or why not? Write three or four paragraphs about art and what it means to your life.

CHAPTER

6 History

Slavery

Icebreaker

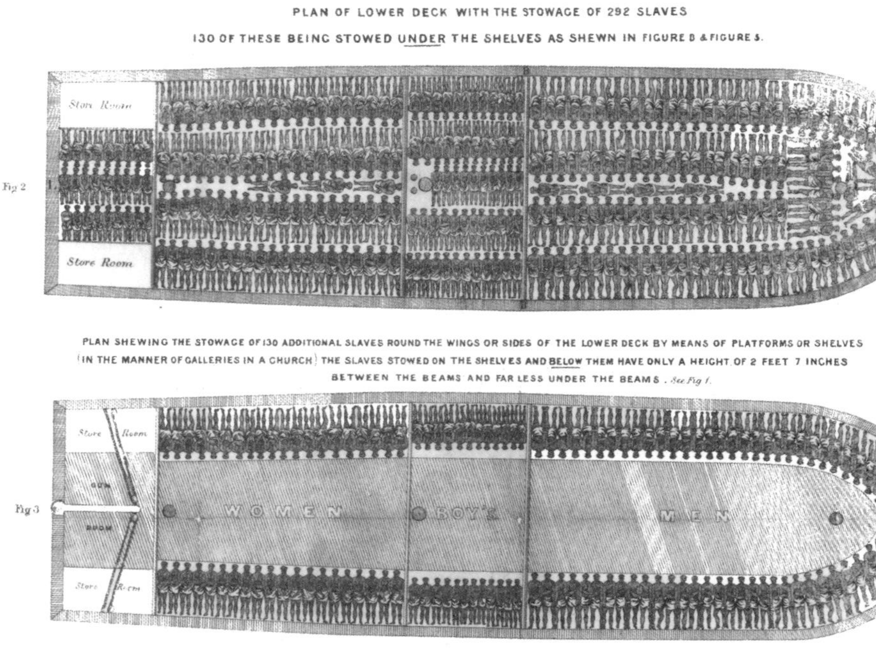

Diagram of a Slave Ship

Discuss these questions with a partner or a group. Write the answers down.

1. Do you enjoy reading about history?
2. Have you seen movies or read stories about slavery? Which ones?
3. Is it important to know about history? Explain your answer.

CHAPTER PREVIEW

What things do you know about the history of slavery? Answer these questions to find out:

1. Do you know where Sierra Leone and Cuba are? *yes* *no*
2. Have you read stories written or told by former slaves? *yes* *no*
3. Would you want to know if your ancestors were slave owners? *yes* *no*

Explain your answer: ______________________________

____

____

____

This chapter presents stories from the history of slavery in Africa and the Americas.

First Step

Vocabulary

These words are found in the reading. Look them up in a dictionary to find their meaning. Write a short sentence for each word, showing its meaning.

Example: kidnap Kidnap means to take another person by force or as a prisoner.

1. *violation:* ______________________________

____

2. *plantation:* ______________________________

____

3. *rebel* (verb): ______________________________

____

4. *captor:* ______________________________

____

5. *steer* (verb): ______________________________

____

6. *current* (noun): ______________________________

____

7. *piracy:* ______________________________

____

8. *abolitionist:* ______________________________

____

9. *heartbroken:* ______________________________

____

Reading

The Amistad Rebellion

"It is time for us to rise, rise up."

On the morning of June 28, 1839, a ship named *La Amistad* ("Friendship") sailed from Havana, Cuba. This was the beginning of an important historical adventure. On this small ship, there were fifty-three Africans who had been kidnapped from West Africa. They were sold, which was a violation of international law.

The buyers wanted to make them slaves on plantations down the coast from Havana. However, their plan failed. On the third day of the ship's voyage, the Africans rebelled. A young farmer from Sierra Leone named Cinque led the rebellion. He wanted to sail the *Amistad* back to Africa.

Cinque directed the *Amistad* east, towards his home. He followed the rising sun—the direction they came from. The Africans made their captors steer the ship. But at night, when Cinque was unable to tell which way was east, the kidnappers sailed north instead. They hoped to take the ship to slave territory along the southeastern part of the United States. So, for two months the *Amistad* sailed east during the day and north during the night.

Finally, on August 25, 1839, the winds and sea currents carried the ship to Long Island, New York. The Africans were put in jail. They were charged with piracy and murder. However, in New York City, a group of abolitionists, led by a man named Lewis Tappan, formed a defense committee for the Africans. Attorney Roger

> Sherman Baldwin received help from the former U.S. President John Quincy Adams. They took the case to the United States Supreme Court, which ruled that the Africans were free.
>
> In 1846, Cinque returned to Africa at last. He was eager to return to his village and find his wife and children. Unfortunately, they were dead, and his village was gone. Cinque was heartbroken, but he did not leave his home. He built a new community and became one of the main rulers of his people.

Check Your Understanding

Choose the correct answer. Check your answer with a classmate or your group.

1. Cinque was
   a. a ship's captain
   b. from West Africa
   c. an abolitionist
   d. from Cuba

2. *La Amistad* was
   a. a slave
   b. a defense committee
   c. a slave ship
   d. a village in Africa

3. John Quincy Adams was
   a. the Cuban president
   b. the ship's captain
   c. a pirate
   d. an American president

4. The people on the ship were sold to be slaves
   a. in Cuba
   b. in the U.S.
   c. in West Africa
   d. in New York

5. The U.S. Supreme Court said that
   a. the Africans were pirates
   b. Cinque had to go to jail
   c. Cinque had to return to Africa
   d. the slaves were free

Group Discussion

Talk about these questions with your group or a partner.

1. What was the plan for the kidnapped Africans?
2. How did the ship finally land in New York?
3. Who helped the Africans gain their freedom?
4. What happened when Cinque returned to Africa?
5. What kind of person was Cinque, in your opinion?

Language Focus: Preposition Practice

Choose the correct preposition for each sentence.

1. *La Amistad* sailed from Havana _______ the morning of June 28.
   a. at
   b. to
   c. of
   d. on

2. This was the beginning _______ an important historical event.
   a. in
   b. at
   c. of
   d. to

3. There were 53 kidnapped Africans _______ the ship.
   a. to
   b. on
   c. of
   d. into

4. Cinque was a young farmer _______ Sierra Leone.
   a. from
   b. to
   c. with
   d. at

5. The kidnappers sailed north _______ night.
   a. to
   b. at
   c. with
   d. on

6. _______ two months, *La Amistad* sailed east during the day.
   a. To
   b. At
   c. With
   d. For

7. The lawyers took the case _______ the U.S. Supreme Court.
   a. at
   b. with
   c. to
   d. in

8. Cinque returned to Africa _______ last.
   a. to
   b. at
   c. with
   d. in

Second Step

Vocabulary

Match the word with its definition. Draw a line to the answer. One has been done for you.

1. *field hand*	a. a mark from an injury
2. *grub* (slang)	b. a superficial injury
3. *flesh wound*	c. food
4. *scar* (noun)	d. food and supplies
5. *muster out* → g	e. retirement income
6. *provisions*	f. someone who works outside on a farm
7. *pension*	g. leave the military

Reading

> **Reading Note:** *The language in this reading reflects a different time in history. There are words and phrases you might not find in a dictionary. They are explained in the column on the right in the reading.*

A Slave's Story

In the 1930s, the U.S. government realized that former slaves were getting old. They wanted to record their stories so they would be remembered forever. They created a project for slaves to be interviewed and recorded. This reading is one interview.

Interviewer: Miss Irene Robertson
Person interviewed: "Soldier" Williams, Forrest City, Arkansas
Age: 98

"My name is William Ball Williams III. I was born in Greensburg. My owners was Robert and Mary Ball. They had four children I knowed. Old man Ball bought ma and two children for one thousand five hundred dollars. I never was

> This is a transcript of spoken speech. The language is not Standard English, so there are many things that look like grammatical errors.

sold. I want to live to be a hundred years old. I'm ninety-eight years old now.

"Ma was Margarett Ball. Pa was William Anderson. Ma was a cook and pa a field hand. They whooped a plenty on the place where I come up. Some of 'em run off. Some they tied to a tree. Bob Ball didn't use no dogs. When they got starved out they'd come outen the woods. Of course they would. Bob Ball raised fine tobacco, fine Negroes, fine horses. He made us go to church. Four or five of us would walk to the white folks' Baptist church. The master and his family rode. It was a good piece. We had dances in the cabins every once in a while. We dance more in winter time so we could turn a pot down in the door to drown out the noise. We had plenty plain grub to eat.

whooped = beat the slaves

where I come up = where I was raised

outen = out of

a good piece = a long way

place a large pot in the doorway to help keep the noise from escaping.

"I run away to Louisville to join the Yankees one day. I was scared to death all the time. They put us in front to shield themselves. They said they was fighting for us—for our freedom. Piles of them was killed. I got a flesh wound. I'm scarred up some. We got plenty to eat. I was in two or three hot battles. I wanted to quit but they would catch them and shoot them if they left. I didn't know how to get out and get away.

The Yankees were the Union Army in the northern United States.

"I mustered out at Jacksonville, Florida and walked every step of the way back. When I got back it was fall of the year. My folks still at my master's. I was on picket guard at Jacksonville, Florida. We fought a little at Pensacola, Florida.

A picket guard watches for the approach of the enemy.

"At the end of the War provisions got mighty scarce. If we didn't have enough to eat we took it. They hadn't raised nothing to eat the last two years. Before I got back to Kentucky the Ku Klux was about and it was hard to get enough to eat to keep traveling on. I was scared nearly to death all the time. I'm not in favor of war. I didn't stay on with the master but my folks lived

He refers here to the Ku Klux Klan.

on. They didn't want to hire Negro soldiers. I traveled about hunting a good place and got to Osceola, Arkansas. I been here in Forrest City twenty odd years. The best people in the world live in Arkansas.

This means more than twenty years, but the number is not precise.

"I'm going to try to go to the Yankee Reunion. They sent me a big letter (invitation). They going to send me a ticket and pay all my expenses. It is at Gettysburg. It is from June 29th to July 6th. My grandson is going to take care of me.

"I get one hundred dollars a month pension. It keeps us mighty well. I want to live to be a hundred years old."

Check Your Understanding

Decide if each statement is *true* or *false.*

1. Bob Ball was the plantation owner.

   true *false*

2. Mr. Williams escaped from slavery.

   true *false*

3. Mr. Williams favored the war.

   true *false*

4. Mr. Williams joined the Confederate army.

   true *false*

5. Mr. Williams' mother was a cook.

   true *false*

6. Mr. Williams walked home after he left the army.

   true *false*

7. Mr. Williams was injured in the war.

   true *false*

8. Mr. Williams was sold as a slave.

   true *false*

9. The Ku Klux Klan made it hard to find food.

   true *false*

10. There was enough food at the end of the war.

   true *false*

Group Discussion

Talk about these questions with your group or a partner.

1. What was Mr. Williams' attitude toward war?
2. What was life like for slaves under Master Ball?
3. What was life like at the end of the Civil War?
4. How did the Ku Klux Klan make it difficult to find food, in your opinion?
5. What is the *Yankee Reunion?*

Language Focus: Spoken and Written Language

As explained before the reading, this interview was a spoken one. If written formally in Standard English, several changes would be made. Look at the statement made by Mr. Williams, and then change it into Standard written English. The first one has been done for you.

1. My owners was Robert and Mary Ball. My owners were Robert and Mary Ball.
2. They had four children I knowed. ______________________________

   ____

3. Some of 'em run off. ______________________________

4. Bob Ball didn't use no dogs. ______________________________

5. I run away to Louisville to join the Yankees one day. ____________

____

6. They said they was fighting for us—for our freedom. ____________

____

7. My folks still at my master's. ______________________________

8. They hadn't raised nothing to eat the last two years. ____________

____

9. I been here in Forrest City twenty odd years. ________________

____

10. They going to send me a ticket and pay all my expenses. _________

____

Third Step

Vocabulary

These words are in the reading. Find them in an English-English dictionary. Discuss their definition with a classmate or your teacher. Write the meanings, and in your own words, write a sample sentence that shows you understand the meaning. (See page 12 for an example.)

1. *hone:* ______________________________________

____

Sample sentence: ______________________________

____

2. *taboo:* ______________________________

____

Sample sentence: ______________________________

____

3. *contemplate:* ______________________________

____

Sample sentence: ______________________________

____

4. *psychoanalysis:* ______________________________

____

Sample sentence: ______________________________

____

5. *latter-day:* ______________________________

____

Sample sentence: ______________________________

____

6. *intangible:* ______________________________

____

Sample sentence: ______________________________

____

7. *pedigreed:* ______________________________

____

Sample sentence: ______________________________

____

8. *culpable:* ______________________________

____

Sample sentence: ______________________________

____

9. *legacy:* ______________________________

____

Sample sentence: ______________________________

____

10. *progeny:* ______________________________

____

Sample sentence: ______________________________

____

Reading

Slaves in the Family

by Edward Ball

About the Author: Edward Ball was born in Georgia and graduated from Brown University in the United States. His ancestors were slave owners. He wrote Slaves in the Family *to tell the experience of finding and meeting the descendants of his family's slaves.* Slaves in the Family *won the National Book Award in 1998.*

When I was a child, Dad used to tell stories about our ancestors, the rice planters. I got a personal glimpse of the American Revolution, because the Balls had played a role in it—some of us fought for the British, some for independence. The Civil War seemed more real since Dad's grandfather and three great-uncles fought for the Confederacy. From time to time in his stories, Dad mentioned the people our family used to own. They were usually just "the slaves," sometimes "the Ball slaves," a puff of black smoke on the wrinkled horizon of the past. Dad evidently didn't know much about them, and I imagine he didn't want to know.

"Did I ever tell you about Wambaw Elias Ball?" he might say. "His plantation was on Wambaw Creek. He had about a hundred and fifty slaves, and he was a mean fella."

My father had a voice honed by cigarettes, an antique Charleston accent, and I liked to hear him use the old names.

"Wambaw Elias was a Tory," Dad began. "I mean, he picked the wrong side in the Revolution." When the Revolutionary War reached the South, Wambaw Elias, instead of joining the American rebels, went to the British commander in Charleston, Lord Cornwallis, who gave him a company of men and the rank of colonel. Wambaw Elias fought the patriots and burned their houses until such time as the British lost and his victims called for revenge. The Americans went for Wambaw Elias's human property, dragging off some fifty slaves from Wambaw plantation, while other black workers managed to escape into the woods. Wambaw Elias knew he had no future in the United States and decided to cash in his assets. Eventually he captured the slaves who had run away, sold them, then took his family to England, where he lived for another thirty-eight years, regretting to the last that he had been forced to give up the life of a slave owner.

In the Ball family, the tale of Wambaw Elias and his slaves passed as a children's story.

* * *

The Balls lived side by side with black families for six generations, but the story, as I knew it, was divided in two. On one side stood the ancestors, vivid, serene, proud; on the other their slaves, anonymous, taboo, half human. I knew a lot about the Balls, but I never knew much about the slaves, even though on the plantations black people far outnumbered white. What were their names? How did they live? Who were their loved ones? When did they leave the plantations, and where had their descendants gone? Could their families be found?

* * *

To contemplate slavery—which for most Americans is a mysterious, distant event—was a bit like doing psychoanalysis on myself. Did the plantations form part of my identity? By outward measure, no. The wealth created by the slave system was destroyed, and the latter-day Balls had no inheritance from it. Some of the family had manners, others none; some had money and status, some neither.

But inwardly the plantations lived on. In childhood, I remember feeling an intangible sense of worth that might be linked to the old days. Part of the feeling came from the normal encouragements of parents who wanted their children to rise. An equal part came from an awareness that long ago our family had lived like lords, and that the world could still be divided into the pedigreed and the rootless.

* * *

The subject of the plantations stirred conflicting emotions. I felt proud (how rare the stories!) and sentimental (how touching the cast of family characters!). At the same time, the slave business was a crime that had not fully been acknowledged. It would be a mistake to say that I felt guilt for the past. A person cannot be culpable for the acts of others, long dead, that he or she could not have influenced. Rather than responsible, I felt accountable for what had happened, called on to try to explain it. I also felt shame about the broken society that had washed up when the tide of slavery receded.

* * *

When I finally chose to look into the slave past, I felt a remarkable calm, and the rest of the path seemed clear. To complete the legacy, I would try to find descendants of the slaves. The plantation heritage was not "ours," like a piece of family property, and not "theirs," belonging to black families, but a shared history. The progeny of slaves and the progeny of slave owners are forever linked. We have been in each other's lives. We have been in each other's dreams. We have been in each other's beds. As I prepared to go back to South Carolina, I thought we should meet, share our recollections, feelings, and dreams, and make the story whole.

Check Your Understanding

Write short answers to the following questions. Check your answers with a partner or with your group.

1. What is meant by the "wrong side in the Revolution"?

____

____

2. What happened to Wambaw Elias's "human property"?

3. Why does the author say that the story of Wambaw and his slaves "passed as a children's story"?

4. When the author says, "On one side stood the ancestors, vivid, serene, proud; on the other their slaves, anonymous, taboo, half human," whose opinion is he stating?

5. Why did the author feel both proud and sentimental about his family's history?

6. Why did the author feel responsible for his family's past?

7. What does the author mean by "inwardly the plantations lived on"?

Group Discussion

Talk about these questions with your group or a partner.

1. Do you agree with the author's opinion that "a person cannot be culpable for the acts of others, long dead, that he or she could not have influenced"?

2. Do you know any family secrets? Do you agree they should be kept a secret?
3. What do you know about American slavery? How did you learn it?
4. Are there any family history stories you can share with your classmates?

Language Focus: Time Words and Phrases

You will find the following words and phrases, related to time, in the reading. Locate them in the reading and be sure you understand how to use them. Then, write a sentence about your own experience, using each phrase correctly.

Example: from time to time: From time to time, my family likes to get together to look at photographs of our ancestors and talk about our history.

1. *usually:* ____________________
2. *the past:* ____________________
3. *eventually:* ____________________
4. *for six generations:* ____________________
5. *have no future:* ____________________
6. *a distant event:* ____________________

7. *latter-day* (adj.): ______________________________

____

8. *to live on:* ______________________________

____

9. *at the same time:* ______________________________

____

10. *finally:* ______________________________

____

Chapter Wrap-Up

Speaking Activities

Discussion and Class Reports

1. Meet with students who read the same reading you did. Review the questions at the end of the reading.
2. Think of one question to ask your group about the reading. Take turns asking your questions.
3. Choose someone from your group to give a report to the class. In your report, tell your classmates what you learned from your reading.
4. Show your classmates one or more of the pictures included with your reading. Explain the image to them.
5. Teach students in other groups one important word you learned from this chapter.

Group Discussion

1. Have you seen any movies about historical events? Describe the movie you have seen. Did you enjoy it?

2. Has an historical event affected your family? How?

3. What time period in the past interests you the most? Why?

Writing Ideas

Write a dialogue between Cinque and his captors. Imagine their conversation as they sailed each day.

Using the Internet or a library, read about the life of another slave. (One source of slave narratives is found at: *http://newdeal.feri.org/asn/*). Write a short summary of what you found.

Is there an historical event that has had a large impact on your family? Research this event in the library or on the Internet. Describe the event factually in two to three paragraphs. Then, tell the story as you've heard it in your family. What similarities and differences are there in the two stories?

For Your Journal

What does it mean to be *brave?* Write a description of a time when you feel you acted bravely. What did you do? Why was it brave?

CHAPTER

7 Business

Business Communication

Icebreaker

Discuss these questions with a partner or a group. Write down the answers.

1. Do you like to talk on the telephone? Why or why not?
2. Have you ever had a job? (Or do you have one now?) What did you do?

3. What kind of job would you like in the future?

CHAPTER PREVIEW

What things do you know about business communication? Answer these questions to find out:

1. Do you know what telephone *etiquette* is? *yes* *no*
2. Do you know what elements to put into your résumé? *yes* *no*
3. Do you understand cultural differences in the workplace? *yes* *no*

Explain your answer: ______________________________

____

____

____

This chapter presents information about different kinds of business communication: telephone calls, résumés, and cross-cultural communication in English.

First Step

Vocabulary

These words are found in your reading. Look up each word you don't know, or discuss them with a partner. Fill in each sentence with the correct word.

etiquette	*customer*	*disconnected*
impression	*on hold*	*direct* (verb)
frustrating	*voicemail*	

1. In order to ______________ a call, you must get the caller's name.
2. Another word for *good manners* is ______________.
3. In order to leave a message, sometimes you must ask for someone's

   ______________.

4. It is important to make a good ________________ when speaking on the telephone.
5. Some people find it ________________ when the phone rings five times and no one answers.
6. The secretary put me ________________ while he looked for the correct phone number.
7. While I was waiting for my friend to answer the telephone, I was suddenly ________________.
8. You should always treat a(n) ________________ politely on the telephone.

Reading

Ten Rules of Good Telephone Etiquette

A lot of business communication happens over the telephone. Your telephone etiquette gives a good first impression of you and your company. The following ten rules will help you make a good impression and keep the customers happy.

1. Answer the phone quickly—after the first ring if you can.
2. Keep message pads and pens or pencils near every telephone. It can be frustrating to wait on the telephone while someone searches for something to write with.
3. Speak clearly and confidently, which will make a good impression.
4. Answer the phone politely. Use a phrase like, "Good Afternoon," and then state your name and your company's name. Ask how you can help the caller. This way, customers

know that they have reached the right telephone number. They also know who is speaking, and it gives them a chance to say why they are calling.

5. If the caller asks for someone else, you should announce the caller. In order to announce the caller, it is good to ask, "May I say who is calling?"
6. If you need to leave the telephone for any reason, it is polite to give the caller a choice, by saying, "May I put you on hold or should I call you back?" If you cannot connect the call to another person, use a phrase like, "Ms. Almeda is not available right now, can I take a message or would you like her voicemail?" Or, "Dr. Wong is talking to another patient right now. Would you like to hold or may I take a message?"
7. Never leave a caller on hold for long. Check once every minute, so callers know that they have not been forgotten or disconnected. If the caller has been on hold more than two or three minutes, offer again to take a message. Remember to thank the caller for waiting.
8. When making a call, politely identify yourself and the reason you are calling. This will help the person answering the telephone direct your call quickly and correctly.
9. If you call someone and must leave a message, speak clearly and spell your name. Speak all numbers slowly, especially if you are using voicemail. If you leave a long message, state your name and phone number again at the end of the message. Always say why you are calling.
10. End calls pleasantly, and thank the person for calling. If you made the call, thank the person for speaking with you.

> If you follow these ten easy rules of telephone etiquette, you will make a good impression on your callers, and on your own employer, too.

Check Your Understanding

Write short answers to these questions. Check your answers with a classmate's.

1. When you make a call, what should you tell the person who answers?

 ____

 ____

2. What should you say when you answer the phone?

 ____

 ____

3. What should you keep near each telephone?

 ____

 ____

4. What should you do if you need to leave the telephone?

 ____

 ____

5. Speaking confidently will make a good first ____________.
6. If you leave a voicemail message, what should you do?

 ____

 ____

7. How quickly should you answer the telephone?

____

____

Group Discussion

Talk about these questions with your group or a partner.

1. Why is telephone etiquette important?
2. In your opinion, which rule in the reading is the most important? Why?
3. Have you ever spoken on the telephone to someone with *bad* telephone etiquette? Explain your answer.

Language Focus: Understanding Telephone Etiquette

Read the following telephone conversation. With a partner, rewrite it so that it follows the rules in the reading. Read your new conversation aloud for your group.

Secretary: Hello.
Customer: I need to talk to the manager.
Secretary: I'm going to put you on hold. *(puts the customer on hold for 3 minutes)*
Secretary: She's not here.
Customer: Can I leave a message?
Secretary: Just a minute, I need to find my pen. *(puts the customer on hold again for 2 minutes)*
Secretary: Okay. What's the message?
Customer: *(speaking quickly)* My name is Luther Leone, 555-7495, I need information on my order, number 56879A.
Secretary: I didn't understand that.
Customer: Just give me her voicemail.
Secretary: Okay. *(disconnects the customer)*

Second Step

Vocabulary

These words are found in the reading. Match each word to its correct definition. Write the letter in the blank. The first one has been done for you.

1. *bullet point*	c	a.	possible or prospective
2. *chronological*	______	b.	not required
3. *major*	______	c.	method of listing items
4. *minor*	______	d.	safe, not causing arguments
5. *non-controversial*	______	e.	secondary field of study
6. *optional*	______	f.	in order of occurrence
7. *outdated*	______	g.	work without salary
8. *potential*	______	h.	main field of study
9. *volunteer*	______	i.	old-fashioned

Reading

A Good Résumé

It is estimated that you have only 30 seconds to prove to a potential employer that you deserve a job interview. That is the amount of time the average employer spends reading a résumé. Obviously, it has to be good! Your résumé summarizes your accomplishments, your education, and your work experience.

The following [on page 149] is an outline of a typical *chronological* résumé — that is, a résumé that shows what you have done over a period of time.

Contact Information

At the top of your résumé, you should include your name, address, telephone number(s), and your e-mail address. If you are a college student, you might include a school address as well as a permanent home address.

Objective

This is an *optional* section that you might include if you are new on the job market. It should be a short statement of the type of work you are seeking.

Accomplishments

Some employers look for a section showing your accomplishments and achievements. This section is a short summary of your résumé; identify any accomplishments that will grab the attention of an employer. Summarize your major accomplishments.

Education

In this section, include the names and locations of the school(s) you have attended, including the years you were there as a student. List your college majors, minors, your completed degrees, and any honors or awards you received.

Professional Experience

This section can also be called "Experience, "Work History," or "Employment." "Experience" is broader than "Work History" because it allows you to include important or interesting school or volunteer projects that might show your skills and abilities.

In this part of your résumé, list each company name, your job titles, the dates of your employment, and your major accomplishments. List your experience in *reverse* chronological order, starting with your most recent experience. Use a bullet point format rather than a paragraph format. Don't discuss your job duties or responsibilities. You can talk about those in the interview. Use action verbs when describing your accomplishments.

Other Information

If you have skills that are relevant to your job but do not fit in any of the categories, include it here. This section is optional.

Affiliations/Interests

This section is also optional; include it only if you have space for it and the activities could be seen as valuable to the employer. Items from this section are sometimes used as an icebreaker by interviewers who want to start an interview informally. This section should only include professional memberships and non-controversial activities and interests. Do not list any religious or political activities, unless they are related to the job.

References

Many experts say this section is outdated, but if you have room, you should include it. Include only a sentence saying references are available upon request. Do not include the names of your references on your résumé.

Of course, be sure that you carefully check your spelling and grammar, and ask a friend to look it over before you send it. Finally, if you are answering a job advertisement, be sure you follow all instructions. If the ad instructs you to send your résumé by e-mail, don't send it by postal mail.

Here is an example of a good chronological résumé:

Résumé for Marsha M. Phillips

Contact Information

Marsha M. Phillips	707-555-1234 (home telephone)
1234 Main Street	707-555-1590 (cell telephone)
Springfield, CA 94404	e-mail: mmphillips@mymail.com

Objective

Seeking a position as a Financial Assistant within a challenging environment.

Accomplishments

Graduated third in my class at the University of Nevada, Reno, with a 4.0 grade point average in my major. Won the inter-collegiate future business leaders' advertising plan competition in 1996. Developed an innovative inventory system for R&R Hotels, implemented in their complete chain of 148 hotels.

Education

University of Nevada, Reno
1994–1997
B.A. in Accounting and Finance, Minor in Communications

Professional Experience

R&R Hotels, Reno, NV
2000–2002

Financial Assistant

- Prepared and monitored budgets for three hotels in a local chain.
- Created an efficient system for control of inventory.
- Supervised audits of each hotel, interacting with external auditors to ensure compliance.
- Presented financial reports to the management team on a quarterly schedule.

Desert Hills Sports Center
1997–2000

Accounts Clerk
- Worked with a team preparing and managing the Center's budget.
- Assisted the Account Manager in maintaining membership records.
- Developed a database to manage membership renewals.
- Prepared the promotional budget in 1998 and 1999.

Other Information
Proficient in using spreadsheet, word-processing, and accounting software programs.
Fluent in Spanish. Reading knowledge of French and Dutch.

Affiliations/Interests
Chapter President of local Debate and Speech Club.
Winner of the 2001 award for public speaking.

References
References available upon request.

Check Your Understanding

Choose the correct answer.

1. The average employer spends ________ reading a résumé.
   a. chronological time
   b. less than a minute
   c. too much time
   d. the interview time
2. The Objective and Affiliations/Interests sections are ________.
   a. important
   b. non-controversial
   c. optional
   d. irrelevant

3. A résumé that lists your most recent job first is called a ________ résumé.
    a. chronological
    b. reverse-chronological
    c. objective
    d. work history

4. When talking about your accomplishments, you should use ________.
    a. optional categories
    b. lots of adjectives
    c. contact information
    d. action verbs

5. Which of the following items usually should <u>not</u> be listed on your résumé?
    a. your political affiliation
    b. your volunteer activities
    c. your college major
    d. your e-mail address

6. Which is the correct way to offer job references?
    a. "For references, please contact Mr. Ling, my current employer."
    b. "Attached are my letters of reference."
    c. "References available upon request."
    d. You should not offer job references.

Group Discussion

Talk about these questions with your group or a partner.

1. What are all the ways you can make sure your résumé will grab the attention of an employer?
2. What if you have no work experience? What could you put on your résumé instead, in your opinion?
3. What things would you list in the affiliations/interests section of a résumé? Why might they help you get a job?
4. What things would you list in the other information section of a résumé? Why might they help you get a job?

Language Focus: Preposition Practice

Choose the correct preposition for each blank.

at *by* *for* *in* *with* *to*

1. ________ the section called Professional Experience, you should include all your recent jobs.
2. Be sure you present your résumé ________ your potential employer in a professional manner.
3. If an ad asks you to send your résumé ________ e-mail, be sure to follow directions.
4. If you graduated first ________ your class, be sure you mention it.
5. If you have a skill that does not fit ________ a category, list it ________ Other Information.
6. Include your affiliations only if you have space ________ it.
7. Include your name and address ________ the top of your résumé.
8. List your jobs, starting ________ the most recent one.
9. You should include any skills that are relevant ________ the job that interests you.
10. You should list your experience ________ reverse chronological order.

Third Step

Vocabulary

These words are in the reading. Find them in an English-English dictionary. Discuss their definition with a classmate or your teacher. Write the meanings, and in your own words, write a sample sentence that shows you understand the meaning. (See page 12 for an example.)

1. *stellar:* ______________________________

   ____

   Sample sentence: ______________________________

   ____

2. *assimilate:* ______________________________

   ____

   Sample sentence: ______________________________

   ____

3. *corporate ladder:* ______________________________

   ____

   Sample sentence: ______________________________

   ____

4. *university extension:* ______________________________

   ____

   Sample sentence: ______________________________

   ____

5. *nuance:* ______________________________

   ____

   Sample sentence: ______________________________

   ____

6. *bug* (slang, verb): ______________________________

____

Sample sentence: ______________________________

____

7. *xenophobic:* ______________________________

____

Sample sentence: ______________________________

____

8. *grounds for:* ______________________________

____

Sample sentence: ______________________________

____

Reading

Ask Evelyn

by Evelyn Nussenbaum
From *Business 2.0,* November 2003

Q: I always receive stellar reviews and generous raises, and yet I'm not being promoted as quickly as my peers. Could my heavy foreign accent be to blame?

A: Obviously your messages are getting through. After all, you say you've been getting healthy pay increases. When doesn't a company speak most sincerely with its pocketbook?

If there's a workplace issue related to your communication skills, it probably concerns your style, not your accent. Many immigrants are so nervous about their spoken English that they "often talk too quickly or put up a wall of words," says Silicon Valley presentation coach Billie Shepard, who helps foreign nationals assimilate into the U.S. workplace. From there, the barrier gets bigger: How we receive information, deliver feedback, and even make eye contact differs from country to country. The cultural clashes can lead to hurt feelings and, unfair as it is, slow climbs up corporate ladders.

Try an accent reduction class. I know, I just said the problem goes beyond accents, but many such workshops also address issues like idioms and effective e-mail writing, and you can easily find classes through university extension programs. Or go whole hog with professionals dedicated to addressing issues that could come between U.S. and foreign employees. Take the nuances of management style: "In Malaysia, a manager is like a father. So one who doesn't check on employees frequently is considered to not be doing his job," says Brett Fenwick of Meridian Resources, a San Francisco global consulting firm. But such attention bugs American workers. It's also common for newcomers to act rudely in their attempt to adopt a direct, "Western" style. You see where all of this can go.

Whatever you do, make sure that you're truly open to change. Teachers note that the proudest professionals are frequently the ones who are most resistant to remaking themselves. "A lot of people with Ph.D.s think that because they have a Ph.D., everything should be OK," says Vera Parr, who's taught accent reduction classes at the University of California at Santa Cruz.

If you think all of your messages are getting across and still believe that you're being penalized, the problem could be a xenophobic boss. Prove that you've been denied promotions based on someone's bias and you have grounds for a lawsuit.

Check Your Understanding

Choose the correct answer.

1. Which of the following statements is <u>not</u> true about the letter writer's problem?
   a. The writer has a strong accent.
   b. The writer is content with his/her good job reviews.
   c. The writer receives large salary increases.
   d. The writer is advancing at the same rate as others.

2. Which of the following is a communication problem, according to Billie Shepard?
   a. speaking with an accent
   b. speaking too quickly
   c. making eye contact
   d. hurting someone's feelings

3. According to Brett Fenwick, what causes some "newcomers" to U.S. business to appear to act rudely?
   a. They try to be like a father to employees.
   b. There are too many nuances in their management style.
   c. They try to take on a more Western style of working.
   d. They don't do their jobs.

4. What does the author mean by the phrase "xenophobic boss"?
   a. An employer who is prejudiced against foreign workers.
   b. An employer who is afraid of outside criticism.
   c. An employer who denies promotions to employees.
   d. An employer who pursues lawsuits against employees.

5. According to teachers, what type of people have the most difficult time changing their behavior?
   a. xenophobic bosses
   b. workers with strong accents
   c. Malaysian managers
   d. professional-level workers

Group Discussion

Talk about these questions with your group or a partner.

1. What is the problem that this reading focuses on?

2. What does Evelyn mean when she asks, "When doesn't a company speak most sincerely with its pocketbook?"

3. What does Evelyn mean when she says it's probably the employee's style rather than accent?

4. Do you agree that if the person believes he or she has been denied promotions because of his or her accent there should be a lawsuit? Explain your answer.

Language Focus: Idioms

This reading contains several idiomatic expressions. Show you understand what they mean by writing a sentence using each phrase.

Example: I don't think I'm **getting through** to you; you need to work harder on this project.

1. to speak with one's pocketbook ______________________________

2. to climb the corporate ladder ______________________________

3. to go whole hog ______________________________

4. to bug someone ______________________________

5. to have grounds for something ______________________________

Chapter Wrap-Up

Speaking Activities

Class Reports

1. Meet with students who read the same reading you did. Review the questions at the end of the reading.
2. Think of one question to ask your group about the reading. Take turns asking your questions.

3. Choose someone from your group to give a report to the class. In your report, tell your classmates what you learned from your reading.

4. Teach students in other groups one important word you learned from this chapter.

Discussion

1. Have you ever applied for a job? Describe your experience.
2. Do you prefer to work indoors or outdoors? Why?
3. In your opinion, what is the best job in the world? Why?
4. Do you like to work with people or by yourself? Why?

Writing Ideas

Imagine you are checking your boss's voicemail. You hear this message:

> *This is Mr. Tom Fredericks from ABC Company. I am calling for Ms. Toyo. I am calling to check on my order. On April 4th, I ordered six chairs, but I got only five of them. You can call me at 555-6712 before 5:00 P.M. today, or tomorrow on my cell phone at 555-1058. I need these chairs, so please call soon.*

Complete this message form, using only the space available. You must shorten the message.

Message for: ____________________
Time: __________ Date: __________
Taken by: ____________________

Name: ____________________
of ____________________
phone number ____________________

___ called ___ stopped by

Please
___ return the call ___ stop by ___ e-mail

Message: ....
....
....
....
....

Write a résumé for a job that you would like. If you don't have any job experience or information to write your résumé now, imagine your résumé ten years from now. What jobs have you had? What degrees have you completed? Write your imaginary résumé for a job in the future.

Imagine you are Evelyn, of *Ask Evelyn,* and you have received the following letter:

> *Dear Evelyn,*
> *I am so excited! My boss asked me to give a big presentation at our sales meeting next week. However, English is not my first language, so I am a little nervous. What should I do to give the best presentation possible?*

Write a response to the letter writer. What advice would you give?

Using the library or the Internet, find information about a job that interests you. What kind of education is needed? What are the main responsibilities? Write a short report about the job you researched.

For Your Journal

If you had all the money you wanted, would you still work? Why or why not?

CHAPTER

8 Geology

Earth's Fury

Icebreaker

Discuss these questions with a partner or a group. Write down the answers.

1. Have you ever been in a terrible storm or earthquake? What was it like?
2. What is your favorite kind of weather?
3. Does any kind of weather scare you? Explain your answer.
4. Would you rather be in an earthquake or a bad storm? Why?

CHAPTER PREVIEW

What things do you know about geology, especially natural disasters? Answer these questions to find out:

1. Do you know what a tornado or cyclone is? *yes* *no*
2. Do you know that scientists can predict earthquakes? *yes* *no*
3. Have you ever heard of Krakatoa? *yes* *no*

Explain your answer: ______________________________

____

____

____

This chapter presents information about different kinds of natural phenomena: tornadoes, earthquakes, and volcanoes.

First Step

Vocabulary

These words are found in the reading. Look them up in a dictionary, and write a short definition in your own words. Draw a picture if it helps you to explain the word.

1. *tornado:* ______________________________

   ____

2. *severe:* ______________________________

   ____

3. *moisture:* ______________________________

   ____

4. *pressure:* ______________________________

____

5. *mass:* ______________________________

____

6. *collide:* ______________________________

____

7. *lightning:* ______________________________

____

8. *hail:* ______________________________

____

9. *detect:* ______________________________

____

10. *shelter:* ______________________________

____

Reading

Reading Note: *Oklahoma is in the center region of the United States. It usually has the second-highest number of tornadoes each year. Texas has the highest number.*

Tornado Hunting

Robert Davies-Jones is a scientist at the National Severe Storms Laboratory in Oklahoma. He studies tornadoes, also called whirlwinds or twisters. To learn about this subject, he must get very close to tornadoes. He goes out in his car to find these storms. He is a scientist, but also a tornado hunter.

In 1994, the U.S. government started a project called VORTEX to gather information about

twisters. Tornado hunters like Davies-Jones put scientific equipment in the path of storms. When a tornado travels past it, the equipment measures its temperature, moisture, air pressure, and speed.

A tornado comes from a huge storm called a *supercell.* This air mass comes from warm air colliding with cooler air. A supercell is several miles wide and up to ten miles high. It can make heavy rain, lightning, hail, and black clouds. A giant whirling wind called a *mesocyclone* forms inside a supercell. The mesocyclone is created by warm air traveling up through cool air, which is moving a different direction. Mesocyclones produce tornadoes.

Modern radar systems can detect mesocyclones. When radar finds a mesocyclone, a tornado warning is sent out so people can take shelter. However, most of the time, mesocyclones do *not* create tornadoes. Scientists want to learn why this is so, in order to predict storms more accurately. They believe they will have more answers after they analyze the VORTEX data.

Tornado Facts

- The average tornado travels for 4–5 miles at a speed of 20–50 miles per hour (mph).
- The average tornado has winds that spin at over 110 mph. They can spin as fast as 250 mph.
- The average tornado is 400–500 feet wide.
- The average tornado lasts only for a few minutes.
- There were 1,235 tornadoes in the U.S. in 2003, killing 51 people.
- Tornadoes are also called cyclones, especially outside of the United States.

Check Your Understanding

Choose the correct answer.

1. How does Robert Davies-Jones hunt tornadoes?
   a. He goes to Oklahoma.
   b. He follows them in his car.
   c. He uses weather equipment.
   d. He uses radar.
2. Which of these things does Davies-Jones' scientific equipment measure?
   a. temperature and moisture
   b. rain and hail
   c. speed and lightning
   d. width and height

3. Which of these things produces tornadoes?
   a. lightning and hail
   b. a mesocyclone
   c. a supercell
   d. radar

4. Which of these things is <u>not</u> produced by a supercell?
   a. hail
   b. dark clouds
   c. warm air
   d. mesocyclones

5. Which of these is not a different name for a tornado?
   a. cyclone
   b. twister
   c. whirlwind
   d. supercell

6. If there is a tornado warning, what should people do?
   a. chase them in their cars
   b. find shelter
   c. get close to it
   d. gather more information

7. How often does a mesocyclone produce a tornado?
   a. always
   b. more than half of the time
   c. less than half of the time
   d. never

Group Discussion

Talk about these questions with your group or a partner.

1. What does a tornado hunter do?
2. What is project VORTEX?
3. Describe the size and speed of a tornado.
4. What do scientists want to learn with the VORTEX data?
5. What do you find surprising about tornadoes?

Language Focus: Size and Number

Each of these sentences has an *incorrect* phrase expressing size. Underline the incorrect phrase, and rewrite it correctly.

Example: A supercell can be ten mile high. ten miles

1. The wind was blowing 20 mile per hour. ______________________

____

2. Tornadoes can be over 400 foot wide. ______________________

____

3. A tornado usually lasts just a few minute. ______________________

____

4. A supercell is severals miles wide. ______________________

____

5. There were over a thousands tornadoes in the U.S. in 2003.

____

____

6. VORTEX started in 1994. In 2004, it was a ten-year-old project.

____

____

7. Tornadoes can spin over 110 mph. ______________________

____

Second Step

Vocabulary

These words are found in the reading. Fill in the blanks in each sentence with the correct word.

bull's-eye	*fluke*	*probability*
cataclysm	*forecast*	*qualification*
credibility	*geophysicist*	*revamp*
designate	*magnitude*	

Example: Someone who studies geology and physics is called a

__geophysicist______.

1. A disaster might also be called a ____________________.
2. An unusual event or coincidence is called a ____________________.
3. Another name for predicting the weather is to ____________________ it.
4. Another way of saying "on target" is ____________________.
5. If someone is believable, they have ____________________.
6. If something is huge, it has a large ____________________.
7. If there are no restrictions on something, we say it is without ____________________.
8. If there is a 75% chance that something will happen, it is said to have a high ____________________.
9. To improve and rebuild something is to ____________________ it.
10. When we name something, we ____________________ it.

Reading

Reading Note: *Menlo Park is a city south of San Francisco in California.*

Japanese Scientists Predicted Big Quake on Island

by Keay Davidson
From the *San Francisco Chronicle*

Friday, September 26, 2003

Just six months before, Japanese scientists forecast the huge earthquake that hit Japan Thursday, September 25, 2003.

Using techniques broadly similar to those used by U.S. scientists, the Japanese scientists estimated a 60 percent probability of an 8.1 magnitude quake in the vicinity of Japan's Tokachi Plain on the island of Hokkaido over the next 30 years.

A quake measuring 8.0 magnitude hit Thursday within the boundaries of the designated region, a 100-by-150-mile area that the scientists called "Region B," just offshore from the Tokachi Plain.

"This is the bull's-eye," said Ross Stein, a geophysicist at the U.S. Geological Survey office in Menlo Park. "This is a direct hit—I would say that without any qualification. I think we need to say that this looks like a very successful forecast."

The forecast was made in March by the Japanese government's Earthquake Research Promotion Committee. The government formed the committee after the disastrous 1995 earthquake in Kobe, Japan, partly to revamp that nation's long-standing effort to forecast and plan for future quakes.

To date, there has been no successful quake forecast whose credibility is widely accepted by the scientific community. And impressive though this recent forecast may look, Stein cautioned, it would be premature to claim that scientists have figured out how to forecast earthquakes in general. There's always the chance that this one is a fluke.

> Only if scientists continue to make successful earthquake forecasts will they be justified in saying they've finally cracked the age-old problem of anticipating these geological cataclysms, said Stein, an American authority on Japanese quakes who collaborates with Japanese researchers.

Check Your Understanding

Write short answers to these questions. Check your answers with a partner or your class.

1. When did the Japanese scientists predict the large earthquake?

 ____

 ____

2. What did the scientists predict exactly?

 ____

 ____

3. What is Region B?

 ____

 ____

4. Why did the Japanese government form the Earthquake Research Promotion Committee?

 ____

 ____

5. Why does Stein think it is premature to believe that the Japanese scientists can predict earthquakes?

 ____

 ____

Group Discussion

Talk about these questions with your group or a partner.

1. Why is it important to predict earthquakes?
2. What regions in the world have severe earthquakes?
3. Have you ever experienced an earthquake? Where? What was it like?
4. If you knew there would be an earthquake, what would you do to prepare for it?

Language Focus: Phrases of Time and Location

These phrases are used in the reading. Write a sentence using your own words, showing you can use each phrase correctly.

1. *just six months before:* ____________________

____

2. *in the vicinity of:* ____________________

____

3. *over the next 30 years:* ____________________

____

4. *within the boundaries of:* ____________________

____

5. *just offshore from:* ____________________

____

Third Step

Vocabulary

There are several words you may not know in your reading. Check the ones you do know, and then look up the others. Write a brief definition for each word you don't know. Check your definitions with a partner's.

- ☐ *eruption:* ______________________________
- ☐ *vigor:* ______________________________
- ☐ *deluge:* ______________________________
- ☐ *pumice:* ______________________________
- ☐ *unbridled:* ______________________________
- ☐ *ferocity:* ______________________________
- ☐ *inaudibly:* ______________________________
- ☐ *detonation:* ______________________________
- ☐ *culminate:* ______________________________

☐ *strait:* ______________________________

____

☐ *inundate:* ______________________________

____

☐ *aftermath:* ______________________________

____

Reading

Reading Note: *Krakatoa (Krakatau) volcano lies in the Sunda strait between the islands of Java and Sumatra.*

Krakatoa

by Simon Winchester

About the Author: Simon Winchester is a writer and adventurer who has written for several magazines, including National Geographic. *He has also received awards as a newspaper writer. This is from* Krakatoa: The Day the World Exploded.

Krakatoa's final twenty hours and fifty-six minutes were marked by a number of phases. First, from early afternoon on Sunday until about 7 P.M. there was a series of explosions and eruptions of steadily increasing frequency and vigor. From early evening the ash falls and the deluge of pumice began. By 8 P.M. the water had become the next medium of transmission of the volcanic energy, and as night fell the temper of the sea in the Sunda Strait became one of unbridled ferocity.

Then, just before midnight, a series of air waves—fast-moving, low-frequency shocks sent out invisibly and inaudibly by the detonations—began arriving in Batavia. The time-ball on the astronomical clock down at Batavia's harbor stopped dead at eighteen seconds after 11:32 P.M. because of the ceaseless vibrations. Audible evidence of the explosions began to radiate outward too, and there was a report from Singapore and Penang that thudding sounds could be heard at about the same time. In Batavia a large number of people, kept awake by the explosions and for want of something better to do, were walking around the Koningsplein;* they noticed that the gas lanterns suddenly dimmed at about 1:55 A.M. Along Rijswijk, the main shopping street, several shop windows suddenly and inexplicably shattered at about the same time.

Then at about 4 A.M. the nature of the explosions reportedly changed, very slightly, becoming less continuous but more explosive. Someone described the sounds as like a steam-engine, emitting full-throated *whoomphs* as it gathered speed. At about 4:56 A.M. an enormously powerful air wave was detected at the Batavia gasworks—suggesting, if travel time over the ninety miles to the volcano is allowed for, that something else had just happened deep within Krakatoa's heart. The culminating explosion—though no one on the ground at the time knew it—was soon to happen.

There were four gigantic explosions still to come. The first was noted at 5:30 A.M. The Sumatran town of Ketimbang was then destroyed at 6:15 A.M., and Anjer, its Javan sister port across the strait—according to the few who survived to tell the tale—was inundated and wrecked very shortly thereafter. The second mighty explosion came at 6:44 A.M.—forty-one minutes after a dawn that, to those in all of western Java, never arrived that day. Ashes began to fall on Batavia, and many of the buildings started to make what were described as "crackling" noises. And then finally, at 10:02 A.M., came the culminating, terrifying majesty of it all.

In the aftermath of Krakatoa's eruption, 165 villages were devastated, 36,417 people died, and uncountable thousands were injured—almost all of them, villages and inhabitants, were victims not of the eruption directly but of the immense sea-waves that were propelled outward from the volcano by that last night of detonations.

* This is Dutch for the "King's Square."

Check Your Understanding

Complete the outline of the last day in the life of Krakatoa. Summarize the events as they happened, using your own words.

Early afternoon, Sunday until 7 P.M. There was a series of explosions that were growing in strength and frequency. Ashes and pumice begin to fall.

8 P.M. ______________________________

11:32 P.M. ______________________________

Just before midnight: ______________________________

1:55 A.M. ______________________________

4 A.M. ______________________________

4:56 A.M. ______________________________

5:30 A.M. ______________________________

6:15 A.M. ______________________________

6:44 A.M. ______________________________

10:02 A.M. ______________________________

Group Discussion

Talk about these questions with your group or a partner.

1. Why did the clock stop in Batavia?
2. What caused the death and injury of so many people?
3. Why were people out walking around past one in the morning?
4. Had you ever heard about Krakatoa before? Explain your answer.

Language Focus: Understanding Complex Language

This writer uses complex language in several places. Reread these sentences and write them in simpler language. Why do you think the author uses more complex phrases?

1. By 8 P.M. the water had become the next medium of transmission of the volcanic energy, and as night fell the temper of the sea in the Sunda Strait became one of unbridled ferocity.

   ____

   ____

   ____

2. Audible evidence of the explosions began to radiate outward too, and there was a report from Singapore and Penang that thudding sounds could be heard at about the same time.

   ____

   ____

   ____

3. The culminating explosion—though no one on the ground at the time knew it—was soon to happen.

   ____

   ____

   ____

4. The Sumatran town of Ketimbang was then destroyed at 6:15 A.M., and Anjer, its Javan sister port across the strait—according to the few who survived to tell the tale—was inundated and wrecked very shortly thereafter.

5. In the aftermath of Krakatoa's eruption, 165 villages were devastated, 36,417 people died, and uncountable thousands were injured—almost all of them, villages and inhabitants, were victims not of the eruption directly but of the immense sea-waves that were propelled outward from the volcano by that last night of detonations.

Chapter Wrap-Up

Speaking Activities

Class Reports

1. Meet with students who read the same reading you did. Review the questions at the end of the reading.
2. Think of one question to ask your group about the reading. Take turns asking your questions.
3. Choose someone from your group to give a report to the class. In your report, tell your classmates what you learned from your reading.
4. On the Internet or in the library, look up more information about the topic of your reading. Include information about your topic (tornadoes, earthquakes, or volcanoes) in your report.

5. Teach students in other groups one important word you learned from this chapter.

Discussion

1. There is a saying, "Everyone talks about the weather, but no one does anything about it." Why is the weather a popular topic of discussion, in your opinion?
2. Does the weather change your mood or feelings? Explain your answer.
3. Would you enjoy seeing a live volcano? Explain your answer.
4. Have you seen any movies about natural disasters? Which ones? Describe the movies to your classmates.

Writing Ideas

Write one or two paragraphs describing how tornadoes are formed and their characteristics.

If you have experienced an earthquake, describe what it was like. If you haven't, find someone who has and interview that person about his or her experience. Write a summary of your interview.

Imagine you were present and could see the destruction of Krakatoa. Write a short story, describing what you see and experience as Krakatoa explodes.

Look at a recent newspaper. What natural disasters are described? Read and summarize a story about a current natural disaster.

For Your Journal

Describe the natural dangers that threaten the area where you live. Are there earthquakes, hurricanes, floods, or other events that sometimes damage your city or area? Have they affected you personally in any way?

CHAPTER

9 Nutrition

Kitchen Science

Icebreaker

Discuss these questions with a partner or a group. Write down the answers.

1. Do you like to eat in restaurants?
2. Do you like to cook?
3. Do you have a healthy diet?
4. What is your favorite thing to eat?
5. What don't you like to eat at all?

CHAPTER PREVIEW

What things do you know about food, especially cooking and nutrition? Answer these questions to find out:

1. Do you know how many vegetables you should eat every day? *yes* *no*
2. Do you know why some foods are called fruits and others are called vegetables? *yes* *no*
3. Do you know anything about the history of restaurants? *yes* *no*

Explain your answer: ______________________________

____

____

____

This chapter presents information about the food we eat: nutrition, fruits and vegetables, and the history of diet and restaurants.

First Step

Vocabulary

Choose the correct word to fit into the blanks. These words are found in your reading.

cereal	*minerals*
container	*vegetarian*
cucumber	*vitamins*
leafy	

1. Someone who does not eat meat is called a ____________________.
2. Something that holds food is called a ____________________.

3. A vegetable that is green on the outside and white inside is called a

   ____________________.

4. For breakfast, many people eat ____________________ with milk.
5. Lettuce and spinach are ____________________ vegetables.
6. Fruit and vegetables are filled with ____________________ and

   ____________________, which are good for you.

Reading

5+ a Day

Every day, you should eat five to nine servings of fruits and vegetables. These foods contain important vitamins and minerals and help you to stay healthy. But, what is a serving? A serving is a medium-sized piece of fruit, six ounces of fruit or vegetable juice, one-half cup of fruit or cooked vegetables, one cup of raw leafy vegetables, one-half cup of cooked peas or beans, or one-quarter cup of dried fruit.

It's easy to eat 5+ a day. Start your morning with some fruit or vegetable juice. Slice some fruit on a bowl of cereal. Eat a green salad with your lunch, and an apple or a pear for your afternoon snack. Cook some beans or carrots

English Measurement	Metric (approximate)
6 ounces	175 ml.
1/2 cup	120 ml.
1/4 cup	60 ml.
1 cup	235 ml.

for dinner, and you already have five servings. If you want to have more than five, add a piece of fruit for a snack or an extra vegetable for dinner.

You can keep your diet interesting by mixing fruits and vegetables of different flavors and colors, like red grapes with bananas, or cucumbers and red tomatoes. Keep fruits and vegetables where you can see them, too. Put fruit in a bowl on the table, and vegetables in clear containers. When you see them, you'll eat them.

Of course, you can get your 5+ at restaurants, too. Try these healthy choices:

- vegetarian pizza
- pasta with vegetables
- vegetable soup
- salad

Try out some new vegetables and fruits, too. Look around at the market and choose something you haven't eaten before. This will help you from getting bored with the same choices. When you get into the habit of eating lots of fruit and vegetables, you might be surprised how good it tastes to stay healthy.

Check Your Understanding

Choose the correct answer.

1. Which of these is not a serving?
   a. one-half cup of beans
   b. one-quarter cup of dried fruit
   c. a medium-size piece of fruit
   d. a cup of vegetable juice

2. How can you make eating fruits and vegetables more interesting, according to the reading?
   a. Slice fruit on your cereal.
   b. Eat more beans and peas.
   c. Mix different flavors and colors.
   d. Eat two fruit snacks every day.

3. Why should you put fruit in a bowl on the table?
   a. It keeps it fresher than in the refrigerator.
   b. You will eat it more often, because you can see it.
   c. It improves the vitamins and minerals in it.
   d. That's where restaurants put their fruit.

4. Why should you try new fruits and vegetables?
   a. It will help you break bad habits.
   b. You will be surprised about it.
   c. You won't get bored with your choices.
   d. You can make vegetarian pizza with them.

5. Which meal does not provide at least two servings of vegetables and fruit?
   a. Breakfast: cereal with 1/2 cup of bananas; 6 ounces of orange juice
   b. Lunch: a pizza with 1/2 cup of peppers and tomatoes, two cups of salad with cucumbers
   c. Snack: one cup of sliced mixed fruit
   d. Dinner: 1/4 cup of cooked carrots, 1/4 cup of peas, chicken

Group Discussion

Talk about these questions with your group or a partner.

1. Do you eat 5+ servings of fruit and vegetables every day? Why or why not?
2. Which vegetable do you dislike? Why?
3. What other things should you eat to stay healthy?
4. Which foods are not healthy for you?

Language Focus: Fruit and Vegetable Words

What words about fruit, vegetables, and eating can you name in this photograph, or from your memory? List them here. The first one has been done for you.

1. eggplant	2.	3.	4.
5.	6.	7.	8.
9.	10.	11.	12.
13.	14.	15.	16.

Second Step

Vocabulary

Complete these statements.

Example: Name something that is *edible:* banana

1. Define the word *tuber:* ______
2. Describe an *artichoke:* ______
3. Describe *chard:* ______
4. If you say something *emphatically,* you say it ______.
5. Something that is *subterranean* is found ______.
6. Describe *rhubarb:* ______
7. If something is *vague,* it is ______.
8. If something is *irreparably* harmed, it ______.
9. Name a food that is high in *acidity:* ______
10. Give an example of *stone fruit:* ______

Reading

Reading Note: *If you aren't familiar with some of the fruits and vegetables named in the reading, you can find pictures of them at:* www.foodpix.com. *Type the name of a fruit or vegetable in the search box to see a picture of it.*

The Difference between Fruits and Vegetables

by Russ Parsons

Both fruits and vegetables come from plants, of course. But what makes one part of a plant a fruit and another a vegetable? Technically, fruits are the seeds and ovaries of plants. Vegetables are any edible parts of plants that are not fruits. In other words, vegetables are leaves, stems, roots (though some parts that grow underground are actually classified as tubers or bulbs) and even, in the case of artichokes, flower buds. Vegetables are not necessarily all of one thing or another. Though spinach is clearly mainly a leaf, chard is emphatically both a leaf and a stem. And sometimes things are not what they seem. Radishes, carrots and turnips are roots, but a potato is not, even though it grows underground. A potato is a swollen subterranean stem (its roots are in its eyes!). In the kitchen, though, the difference between fruits and vegetables is not as clear-cut as in science. We tend to call plant parts that are not distinguished by a noticeable sweetness vegetables. Therefore, while such things as tomatoes, cucumbers, green beans and peppers are all technically fruits, culinarily* they are treated as vegetables.

Though fruits and vegetables may be similar at the most basic structural level, they're very different in other ways. While many fruits are used as vegetables, only a few vegetables are used as fruits (rhubarb, a stem, is one of them). The biggest difference between fruits and vegetables is that with vegetables, ripeness is usually considered automatic (one reason that it's important to remember that tomatoes are

* "Culinarily" is a form of the word "culinary" or related to cooking.

actually fruits). With fruits, ripeness is highly variable and critical. It is also vague.

Here are five tips for using fruits and vegetables:

- Buying the best ingredients is the real key to vegetable cookery. Pick those that are heaviest for their size and have the firmest texture. Bright colors are another good indicator of freshness.
- Once you get vegetables home, they should go straight into the refrigerator. The only exception is the tomato, which is a fruit, not a vegetable. Never refrigerate tomatoes. Their flavors will be irreparably damaged.
- Buy the following fruits fully ripe: berries, cherries, grapes, watermelon and citrus. All except berries can be refrigerated without losing flavor.
- Most fruits that are cooked need a little acidity such as citrus juice, not only to brighten their flavors but to maintain their color.
- If you buy stone fruit and pears that are hard, you can ripen them by storing them at room temperature in a closed paper bag. Adding an apple will speed the process.

Check Your Understanding

Mark whether these statements are *true* or *false.*

1. An artichoke is a flower bud.

   true *false*

2. Potatoes are a root vegetable.

   true *false*

3. Technically, a cucumber is a vegetable.

   true *false*

4. The biggest difference between fruits and vegetables is found in its ripeness.

   true *false*

5. Heavy vegetables are low in quality.

   true *false*

6. You should not refrigerate tomatoes.

   true *false*

7. You should buy cherries when they are ripe.

   true *false*

8. Vegetables are the stems of a plant. Everything else is a fruit.

   true *false*

9. In cooking, the difference between fruits and vegetables is sometimes ignored.

   true *false*

10. Green beans are a fruit often used as a vegetable.

    true *false*

Group Discussion

Talk about these questions with your group or a partner.

1. Do you prefer to eat fruit or vegetables? Explain your answer.
2. What is one surprising thing you learned from the reading? Why was it surprising?
3. Is there a fruit or vegetable that is connected to your culture or home country? Why is it important?

Language Focus: Fruit and Vegetable Words

There are a lot of names for fruits and vegetables. How many do you know? For each letter of the alphabet listed below, write the name of one fruit or vegetable, and check the box to show which it is, a fruit or vegetable. Can you fill all the spaces?

Name	Fruit?	Vegetable?
Example: Apple ____	X	
1. B ____		
2. C ____		
3. D ____		
4. F ____		
5. G ____		
6. I ____		
7. L ____		
8. M ____		
9. N ____		
10. O ____		
11. P ____		
12. R ____		
13. S ____		
14. T ____		
15. W ____		

Third Step

Vocabulary

These words are found in the reading. Check the ones you know. Write a short definition for each.

☐ *banquet:* ____

____

☐ *puree:* ____

____

☐ *meat stock:* ____

____

☐ *mulled:* ____

____

☐ *bouillon:* ____

____

☐ *ubiquitous:* ____

____

☐ *gruel:* ____

____

☐ *laud:* ____

____

☐ *panacea:* ____

____

☐ *acrimony:* ____

____

☐ *dire:* ______________________________

____

☐ *periphery:* ______________________________

____

☐ *entrepreneur:* ______________________________

____

☐ *gastronomic:* ______________________________

____

☐ *quintessence:* ______________________________

____

☐ *well-heeled:* ______________________________

____

Reading

The First Restaurants

by Rachel Laudan

About the Author: Rachel Laudan is the author of The Food of Paradise: Exploring Hawaii's Culinary Heritage, *which was the winner of the 1997 Julia Child* Cookbook Award for Distinguished Scholarship.*

Were we to attend a 16th century court banquet in France or England, the food would seem strange indeed to anyone accustomed to traditional Western cooking. Dishes might include blancmange—a thick puree of rice and chicken moistened with milk from ground almonds, then sprinkled with sugar and fried pork fat. Roast suckling pig might be accompanied by a cameline sauce, a side dish made of sour grape juice thickened with bread crumbs, ground

* Julia Child was a famous American chef who appeared on many television cooking programs in the United States. She died in 2004.

raisins and crushed almonds, and spiced with cinnamon and cloves. Other offerings might consist of fava beans cooked in meat stock and sprinkled with chopped mint or quince paste, a sweetmeat of quinces and sugar or honey. And to wash it all down, we would probably drink hypocras, a mulled red wine seasoned with ground ginger, cinnamon, cloves and sugar.

Fast-forward 100 years, though, and the food would be reassuringly familiar. On the table might be beef bouillon, oysters, anchovies and a roast turkey with gravy. These dishes might be served alongside mushrooms cooked in cream and parsley, a green salad with a dressing of oil and vinegar, fresh pears, lemon sherbet, and sparkling white wine. Before 1650, the elite classes throughout the Islamic and Christian worlds from Delhi to London shared pretty much the same diet: thick purees, lots of spices, sweet and sour sauces, cooked vegetables, and warmed wines. Sugar was ubiquitous as a seasoning in savory dishes. But in the middle of the 17th century, the northern European diet began to change. This new regimen relied on fewer spices, based its sauces on fats such as butter and olive oil, and incorporated raw fruits and vegetables. Sugar appeared only at the end of a meal. What happened? Economic considerations cannot account for the difference: for the upper class, money was no object. For the poor, both meals would have been far out of reach. Well into the 19th century, they subsisted on vegetable soups and gruels with bread or porridge. Novel foodstuffs from the New World do not explain the shift in diet either, because with the exception of turkey, the dishes at the second banquet depended not on new ingredients but on new uses of long familiar ones. The clue to this transformation in eating habits between the 16th and 17th centuries must be sought instead in evolving ideas about diet and nutrition—which is to say, in the history of chemistry and medicine.

As fruits, herbs and vegetables assumed a more prominent place in the main meal, sugar, formerly lauded as a panacea, came in for rough treatment at the hands of the chemical physicians. Some wanted to banish it altogether. "Under its whiteness," hissed Joseph Duchesne, physician to Henry IV of France, in 1606, "sugar hides a great blackness"—doctors knew that it blackened the teeth—"and under its sweetness a very great acrimony, such that it equals *agua fortis* [nitric acid]."

The moral was clear: sugar was dangerous, perhaps even a poison. Such dire warnings would surely have given any chef second thoughts about sprinkling it over the main dishes of the meal, leaving the diner no choice but to eat it. Thus, sugar moved to the periphery of the menu, served only in desserts, which were prepared in a separate kitchen. Sugar became the subject of a distinct genre of books dedicated to its decorative, not medical, properties.

Chefs made essences of meat or fish from the "musculous Flesh, which is of all [parts of the animal] the most nourishing, that which produces the best juice," and then served this healthy fare in the form of stock, bouillon or jellies made from these liquids. Land animals had more nutritious juices than fish or birds did, and of the land animals, beef produced the most restorative ones. Before long, entrepreneurs saw an opportunity in this new cuisine, selling "restaurants"—which is French for "restoratives"—to those who could not afford their own chefs.

Eventually Europe's middle classes emulated the aristocracy, developing a taste not only for restaurants but for all the new cuisine. Such foods seemed to offer a certain refinement, not just in the sense of good taste but also in a chemical sense, as the meals represented the most enhanced form of food. As the authors of the gastronomic treatise *The Gifts of Comus,* published in Paris in 1739, put it: "Modern cookery is a kind of chemistry. The cook's science consists today of analyzing, digesting, and extracting the quintessence of foods, drawing out the light and nourishing juices, mingling and blending them together."

This new diet gradually spread across Europe as it simultaneously made its way down the social scale. By the mid to late 19th century it had become the standard for the English- and French-speaking worlds in Europe, the U.S., Canada and Australia.

The Western cuisine born in the 17th century long outlived the dietary theory that inspired it. By the end of the 18th century, chemists and physicians had embarked on the research that was to lead to the modern theories of the role of calories, carbohydrates, proteins, vitamins and minerals in the biochemical processes of digestion. Notably, during the 19th and early 20th centuries, when most of these studies were carried out, nutritionists focused on developing a cheap but adequate diet for factory workers, soldiers and other less affluent people. The shift of emphasis in the medical community from the rich to the poor, though, meant that chefs catering to the well-heeled continued to develop Western cuisine along the lines established in the 17th century.

> Now that almost everyone in the West can afford the cuisine formerly restricted to the wealthy, we have come to realize that its dietary foundations are a mixed blessing. Although fresh fruit and vegetables score high marks, the centrality of fat in our diets (a result of the importance given to meat and fat-based sauces) is blamed for the high rates of obesity in most developed nations. In response, everyone from physicians to chefs has returned attention to the age-old problem of developing a new cuisine, at once delicious and in line with the latest findings in physiology and nutrition.

Check Your Understanding

Write short answers to the following questions. Check your answers with a partner or your group.

1. What is *blancmange?*

 ____

 ____

2. What is *hypocras?*

 ____

 ____

3. Before 1650, what was the Western diet like?

 ____

 ____

4. How was sugar used in the diet before 1650?

 ____

 ____

5. How did food from the New World affect the change in the Western diet, according to the reading?

 ____

 ____

6. Why does the author say that the dietary foundations of Western cuisine are a "mixed blessing"?

____

____

7. What is a *restaurant,* according to the reading?

____

____

Group Discussion

Talk about these questions with your group or a partner.

1. Describe one thing you learned from this reading that you found interesting.
2. Is your diet similar to, or different from, the modern diet described in the reading? Explain your answer.
3. What was the attitude toward sugar in the 1600s? Is it the same as or different from current attitudes toward sugar? Explain your answer.
4. Do you prefer to eat in restaurants or at home? Why?

Language Focus: Article Practice

Decide which article (*a, an, the,* or nothing) belongs in each of the blanks. In some cases, more than one choice is possible. Be prepared to discuss your answers. The first one has been done for you.

If you went to ___a___ banquet in _______ (1) Western Europe in 1600, _______ (2) meal would seem strange if you were used to _______ (3) modern Western diet. _______ (4) meals might offer _______ (5) thick puree of ________ (6) rice and ________ (7) chicken made with ________ (8) milk from ________ (9) ground almonds, and then sprinkled with ________ (10) sugar. Other dishes might include ________ (11) Italian beans cooked in ________ (12) meat stock and sprinkled with ________ (13) chopped mint. You would probably drink ________ (14) hypocras, ________ (15) warm red wine seasoned with ________ (16) ground ginger, ________ (17) cinnamon, ________ (18) cloves and ________ (19) sugar.

Chapter Wrap-Up

Speaking Activities

Class Reports

1. Meet with students who read the same reading you did. Review the questions at the end of the reading.
2. Think of one question to ask your group about the reading. Take turns asking your questions.
3. Choose someone from your group to give a report to the class. In your report, tell your classmates what you learned from your reading.
4. Find a food site on the Internet (for example, *www.foodtv.com*) or a cookbook in the library. Find a recipe that interests you, and present it to your class. Would it be easy or difficult to prepare?
5. Teach students in other groups one important word you learned from this chapter.

Discussion

1. What is your favorite dish? How do you make it? Describe it to the class.
2. Would you enjoy a job at a restaurant? Why or why not?
3. What holidays do you enjoy by celebrating with food? What dishes are important to that holiday?

Writing Ideas

Write two paragraphs explaining why it is important to eat fruits and vegetables every day.

Write two to three paragraphs about your favorite dish—what is in it, and how is it made? Is it simple to cook, or difficult?

On the Internet or in your library, locate information about the diet of a culture that is unfamiliar to you. For example, what do they eat in Iceland, Kenya, or Paraguay? Write a one-page essay about what you learned.

What is your favorite restaurant? Write a short review of the restaurant, and recommend it to a friend. What is the best dish? What kind of food do they serve? Is the service friendly? Be sure to include its address, if you know it.

For Your Journal

How important is food in your daily life? Do you "eat to live" or "live to eat"? Describe your food habits.

CHAPTER

10 Ecology

Heroes for the Environment

Icebreaker

Discuss these questions with a partner or a group. Write down the answers.

1. Do you recycle bottles or paper? Why or why not?
2. Are you concerned about the environment? Explain your answer.
3. Does your school or workplace recycle? If they do, describe the recycling program.

CHAPTER PREVIEW

What things do you know about people who protect our environment? Answer these questions to find out:

1. Do you know who Jacques Cousteau was? *yes* *no*
2. Have you heard of the American writer John Steinbeck? *yes* *no*
3. Are you familiar with the book *Silent Spring* or its author, Rachel Carson? *yes* *no*

Explain your answer: ____________________

____

____

____

This chapter presents information about people who have worked for environmental causes: Jacques Cousteau, John Steinbeck, and Rachel Carson.

First Step

Vocabulary

Answer these questions. The words in *italics* are in your reading.

1. Name three things that are found *underwater:*

   ____________, ____________, and

   ____________.

2. Describe an *aqualung.* ____________________
3. Give another word for *apparatus.* ____________________
4. Describe what a *diver* does. ____________________

5. If you *finance* something, you ______________________________ it.

6. Describe what *dolphins* look like. ______________________________

7. Name three popular *TV series:* ____________________,

____________________, and ____________________.

8. What is a *coral reef?* ______________________________

9. If something *shrunk,* what happened to it? ____________________

Reading

Reading Note: *The name Jacques Cousteau is French and pronounced "zhock coo-stow."*

Jacques Cousteau

Jacques-Yves Cousteau was born in France on June 11, 1910. His parents were Daniel and Elizabeth Cousteau. Cousteau always loved the water. In his early teenage years, he also became interested in machines and films. He saved his money and bought a movie camera.

After high school, Cousteau entered the Naval Academy.* In 1933, he joined the French Navy. During this time, he began his underwater explorations and also started to work on an underwater breathing machine. In 1943, he and a French engineer named Emile Gagnan completed the *aqualung,* usually called SCUBA (**s**elf-**c**ontained** **u**nderwater **b**reathing **a**pparatus). This equipment allows a diver to stay underwater for several hours.

In 1950, Cousteau purchased the ship *Calypso* for his explorations. To help finance his voyages and increase public awareness of his undersea work, Cousteau made films and

* The Naval Academy is a college for students who will become officers in the navy.

** "Self-contained" means that something works by itself, without help.

published books. His films include *The Silent World* (1956) and *World without Sun* (1966). His books include *The Living Sea* (1963), *Dolphins* (1975), and *Jacques Cousteau: The Ocean World* (1985).

In 1968, Cousteau was asked to make a TV series. For eight years, *The Undersea World of Jacques Cousteau* showed the world of whales, sharks, dolphins, and coral reefs. Cousteau's fight for the environment grew stronger as he got older. In the 1960s he talked about the sea as a resource. In 1970, he warned the public that ocean life had shrunk 40 percent in 20 years. In 1974, Cousteau started the Cousteau Society to protect ocean life.

Cousteau died on June 25, 1997, in Paris, France.

Check Your Understanding

Put the events of Jacques Cousteau's life in order. The first one has been done for you.

a. ___1___ He was born June 11, 1910.

b. ________ He bought the ship called the *Calypso.*

c. ________ He died in Paris.

d. ________ He designed the aqualung with his friend Emile Gagnan.

e. ________ He bought his first movie camera.

f. ________ The Cousteau Society was formed.

g. ________ He joined the French Navy.

h. ________ He wrote the book *The Living Sea.*

i. ________ His TV series began.

j. ________ He entered the Naval Academy.

Group Discussion

Talk about these questions with your group or a partner.

1. What kind of person was Jacques Cousteau?
2. Why was Cousteau worried about the ocean?
3. Why did Cousteau make films and write books, according to the reading?
4. Do you enjoy the ocean and sea life? Explain your answer.

Language Focus: Synonyms

Two words that mean the same thing, or nearly the same thing, are called *synonyms.* For example, *big* and *large* are synonyms. Writers use synonyms when they don't want to repeat words. Synonyms help make writing more interesting.

The writer of "Jacques Cousteau" uses synonyms. Can you find them?

Example: bought: purchased

1. *entered:* ____________
2. *started:* ____________
3. *equipment:* ____________
4. *sea:* ____________

Now, think of synonyms for these words from the reading:

5. *allows:* ____________
6. *help:* ____________

Second Step

Vocabulary

These words are found in your reading. Do not look them up now; instead, read the passage by John Steinbeck. As you read, put a check (✓) next to these words as you find them. Try to define them *in context.* Discuss what they mean with a partner after you finish your reading. Make notes next to the words or phrases.

tattered: ____________________________

____

hospitable: ____________________________

____

mirage: ______________________________

____

cove: ______________________________

____

gloom: ______________________________

____

anchor: ______________________________

____

humidity: ______________________________

____

dredging: ______________________________

____

fleet: ______________________________

____

ramifications: ______________________________

____

ascendancy: ______________________________

____

depleted: ______________________________

____

catch limits: ______________________________

____

combed: ______________________________

____

timber: ____

____

prodigal: ____

____

ideologies: ____

____

Reading

> **Reading Note:** *In 1940, John Steinbeck and his friend, biologist Edward Ricketts, sailed a boat out of Monterey, California, in order to explore the wildlife of the Sea of Cortez (Gulf of California). Steinbeck wrote about this trip in the book* The Log from the Sea of Cortez.

The Log from the Sea of Cortez

by John Steinbeck

About the Author: John Steinbeck was born February 27, 1902, in Salinas, California. He studied at Stanford University between 1920 and 1925 but never received a degree. Steinbeck's first novel, Tortilla Flat, *published in 1935, was a huge success. In 1938,* The Grapes of Wrath *was published. This novel is about the difficulties of an Oklahoma family who become farmworkers in California. It won a Pulitzer Prize in 1939. After World War II, Steinbeck became interested in marine biology and published a non-fiction book,* The Log from the Sea of Cortez, *in 1941. Steinbeck won the Nobel Prize for literature in 1962 and the U.S. Medal of Freedom in 1964. He died in New York in 1968.*

April 8, 1940

We sailed out on Monday, a little tattered and a little tired. Captain Corona, pilot and shrimp-boat owner, who had been kind and hospitable to us, piloted us out and stopped one of his incoming boats for us to inspect. It was a poor small boat, and had not much of a catch of shrimps. Everyone in this neighborhood had complained of the Japanese shrimpers who were destroying the shrimp fisheries. We determined to pay them a visit on the next day. The moment we dropped the pilot, just outside of Guaymas, the gulf was local again and part of the design it had put in our heads. The mirage was over the land and the sea was very blue. We sailed only a short distance and dropped our anchor in a little cove opposite the Pajaro Island light. That night we caught a number of fish that looked and felt like catfish. Tex skinned them and prepared them, and we did not eat them. A little gloom hung over all of us; Sparky and Tiny had fallen in love with Guaymas and planned to go back there and live forever. But Tex and Tony were gloomy and a little homesick.*

We were awakened well before daylight by the voices of men paddling out for the day's fishing, and it was with some relief that we pulled up our anchor and started out to continue the work we had come to do. The day was thick with haze, the sun came through it hot and unpleasant, and the water was oily and at the same time choppy. The sticky humidity was on us.

In about an hour we came to the Japanese fishing fleet. There were six ships doing the actual dredging while a large mother ship of at least 10,000 tons stood farther offshore at anchor. The dredge boats themselves were large, 150 to 175 feet, probably about 600 tons. There were twelve boats in the combined fleet including the mother ship, and they were doing a very systematic job, not only of taking every shrimp from the bottom, but every other living thing as well. They cruised slowly along in echelon** with overlapping dredges, literally scraping the bottom clean. Any animal which escaped must have been very fast indeed, for not even the sharks got away. Why the Mexican government should have permitted the complete destruction of a valuable food supply is one of those mysteries which have their ramifications possibly back in pockets it is not well to look into.

* * *

We liked the people on this boat very much. They were good men, but they were caught in a large destructive machine, good men doing a bad thing. With their many and large boats, with their industry and efficiency, but most of all with their intense energy, these Japanese will obviously soon clean out the shrimps of the region. And it is not true that a species thus attacked comes back.

* Tex, Tony, Sparky, and Tiny are all men working on Steinbeck's boat.

** "In echelon" means in the order of importance of boats.

The disturbed balance often gives a new species ascendancy and destroys forever the old relationship.

In addition to the shrimps, these boats kill and waste many hundred of tons of fish every day, a great deal of which is sorely needed for food. Perhaps the Ministry of Marine had not realized at that time that one of the good and strong food resources of Mexico was being depleted. If it has not already been done, catch limits should be imposed, and it should not be permitted that the region be so intensely combed. Among other things, the careful study of this area should be undertaken so that its potential could be understood and the catch maintained in balance with the supply. Then there might be shrimps available indefinitely. If this is not done, a very short time will see the end of the shrimp industry in Mexico.

We in the United States have done so much to destroy our own resources, our timber, our land, our fishes, that we should be taken as a horrible example and our methods avoided by any government and people enlightened enough to envision a continuing economy. With our own resources we have been prodigal, and our country will not soon lose the scars of our grasping stupidity. But here, with the shrimp industry, we see a conflict of nations, of ideologies, and of organisms. The units of the organisms are good people . . . The Mexican official and the Japanese captain were both good men, but by their association in a project directed honestly or dishonestly by forces behind and above them, they were committing a true crime against nature and against the immediate welfare of Mexico and the eventual welfare of the whole human species.

Check Your Understanding

Choose the correct answer.

1. What was the Japanese fleet doing?
   a. fishing for sharks
   b. taking shrimp from the water
   c. leaving on the mother ship
   d. being formal and polite

2. Why did Steinbeck say the fishermen were doing a "bad thing"?
    a. they were removing too many shrimp
    b. they had intense energy
    c. they had ascendancy and balance
    d. they didn't care about relationships
3. What is a "catch limit"?
    a. a fish and game official
    b. a food resource
    c. a law about fishing
    d. a scientific study
4. The author believes:
    a. The Japanese were criminals for ruining the environment.
    b. The U.S. destroyed many of its own resources.
    c. The Mexican government was irresponsible.
    d. The fishermen didn't care about the environment.
5. Which of these does not reflect the author's beliefs in this reading?
    a. Overfishing will harm Mexico's future.
    b. People should not fish or eat animals.
    c. Many people and ideas are in conflict over the environment.
    d. Humans will be harmed by their treatment of the environment.
6. What were the Japanese sailors doing to the fish in the area?
    a. killing and wasting them
    b. taking them for food
    c. giving them to the Mexicans
    d. nothing; they were only catching shrimp

Group Discussion

Talk about these questions with your group or a partner.

1. What was Steinbeck's impression of the Japanese fishermen? Explain your answer.
2. Is overfishing a problem today? Explain your answer.

3. What can the government do to protect fish and other sea life?
4. Do you think the environment is in better, or worse, condition than it was in 1940? Defend your answer with examples.

Language Focus: Article Practice

Which article (*a, an, the,* or nothing) goes in each of the blanks? In some cases, more than one choice is possible. Discuss your answers.

In ________ (1) hour they came to ________ (2) Japanese boats. There were twelve boats in ________ (3) fleet including ________ (4) mother ship, and they were doing ________ (5) systematic job, not only of taking every shrimp from ________ (6) bottom, but every other living thing as well. Any animal that escaped must have been very fast, for not even ________ (7) sharks got away. They went up on ________ (8) bridge. They stopped and talked to ________ (9) sailor for ________ (10) few minutes before they realized that he did not speak ________ (11) English. ________ (12) Japanese captain was formal, but courteous. His business was done through ________ (13) interpreter. ________ (14) Mexican fish and game official who was aboard was ________ (15) pleasant man, but he said that he had no information about ________ (16) animals he was overseeing.

Third Step

Vocabulary

These words are found in your reading. Do not look them up now; instead, read the passage. As you read, put a check (✓) next to these words as you find them. Try to define them *in context.* Discuss what they mean with a partner after you finish your reading. Make notes next to the words or phrases.

pesticide: ____________________

____

inanimate: ____________________

____

residue: ____________________

____

contamination: ____________________

____

burrow: ____________________

____

prodigious: ____________________

____

insecticidal: ____________________

____

prewar: ____________________

____

rotenone: ____________________

____

leguminous: ______________________________

____

sinister: ______________________________

____

oxidation: ______________________________

____

malignancy: ______________________________

____

teem: ______________________________

____

validity: ______________________________

____

biodiversity: ______________________________

____

synergistic: ______________________________

____

bioaccumulative: ______________________________

____

herbicide: ______________________________

____

endocrine: ______________________________

____

zoologist: ______________________________

____

deployment: ______________________________

____

Reading

Reading Note: *This reading is actually two separate readings—a short excerpt from the famous book* Silent Spring *by Rachel Carson and a reflection on the issues it raised, forty years later.*

Silent Spring

by Rachel Carson

About the Author: Rachel Carson (1907–1964) wrote about ecology and the environment in her book Silent Spring, *published in 1962. This book is widely believed to have begun the environmental movement. It is considered one of the most important books of the 20th century. The "silent spring" was Carson's metaphor for the destruction of the environment by human beings.*

For the first time in the history of the world, every human being is now subjected to contact with dangerous chemicals, from the moment of conception until death. In the less than two decades of their use, the synthetic pesticides have been so thoroughly distributed throughout the animate and inanimate world that they occur virtually everywhere. They have been recovered from most of the major river systems and even from streams of groundwater flowing unseen through the earth. Residues of these chemicals linger in soil to which they may have been applied a dozen years before. They have entered and lodged in the bodies of fish, birds, reptiles, and domestic and wild animals so universally that scientists carrying on animal experiments find it almost impossible to locate subjects free from such contamination. They have been found in fish in remote mountain lakes, in earthworms burrowing in soil, in the eggs of birds—and in man himself. For these chemicals are now stored in the bodies of the vast majority of human beings, regardless of age. They occur in the mother's milk and probably in the tissues of the unborn child.

All this has come about because of the sudden rise and prodigious growth of an industry for the production of man-made, or synthetic, chemicals with insecticidal properties. This industry is a child of the Second World War. In the course of developing agents of chemical warfare, some of the chemicals created in the laboratory were found to be lethal to insects. The discovery did not come by chance: insects were widely used to test chemicals as agents of death for man.

The result has been a seemingly endless stream of synthetic insecticides. In being man-made—by ingenious laboratory manipulation of the molecules, substituting atoms, altering their arrangement—they differ sharply from the simpler insecticides of prewar days. These were derived from naturally occurring minerals and plant products—compounds of arsenic, copper, lead, manganese, zinc, and other minerals; pyrethrum from the dried flowers of chrysanthemums; nicotine sulphate from some of the relatives of tobacco; and rotenone from leguminous plants of the East Indies.

What sets the new synthetic insecticides apart is their enormous biological potency. They have immense power not merely to poison but to enter into the most vital processes of the body and change them in sinister and often deadly ways. Thus, as we shall see, they destroy the very enzymes whose function is to protect the body from harm, they block the oxidation processes from which the body receives its energy, they prevent the normal functioning of various organs, and they may initiate in certain cells the slow and irreversible change that leads to malignancy.

* * *

Environmental Movement at 40: Is Earth Healthier?

by Hillary Mayell

Forty years ago Rachel Carson, a writer and marine biologist, published *Silent Spring,* a book documenting the chemical warfare that human beings were waging on the natural world.

As she saw it, a small American town, the farms prosperous, the people healthy and happy, the forests teeming with wildlife—all was silenced, or sickened by a mysterious illness brought on by the people themselves. The "strange blight" was caused by the unexamined and virtually unregulated practice of dumping, spraying, dusting, and otherwise distributing harmful chemicals into the environment.

The chemical industry, government scientists, and the media attacked Carson as a hysterical woman; her facts were called inaccurate, her competency questioned. But her book became a best-seller.

Reviewing the book in 1962, *Time* magazine joined the crowd, questioning the book's accuracy and the validity of her conclusions; several decades later, the magazine named her one of the 100 most influential people of the 20th century.

Are we better off since Carson opened the eyes of Americans to the destruction being wreaked on nature?

"I think we are better off in the sense that this is known to be a problem and there is some regulation and even prohibition in some cases," said Thomas E. Lovejoy, chief biodiversity adviser for the World Bank and chair of the Conservation Trust Advisory Board of the National Geographic Society.

"Better off than we would have been," he added. "But we continue to introduce new chemicals to the environment, even new categories of threats, and pre-test them insufficiently. And almost nothing is being done to look at combined and possibly synergistic effects."

Monday, April 22, is Earth Day 2002, and the planet's problems are legion. Research and political maneuvering in recent decades suggest that now, more than ever, revisiting Rachel Carson may be imperative.

Persistent Toxins

Carson was the first to introduce the general public to the concept of persistent bioaccumulative toxins—substances that are long lasting, move readily from land to air and water, and can build up in the food chain to levels that are harmful to humans, wildlife, and the environment. These compounds can be found everywhere—in herbicides, pesticides, insecticides, detergents, plastics, and even cosmetics.

When Carson wrote her book, toxicity testing of new chemical compounds was limited to figuring out whether exposure to a chemical at high concentrations would cause cancer. Since then, scientists have discovered a previously unsuspected threat posed by many synthetic chemicals: the ability to disrupt the body's internal chemical messaging systems.

Even at very low levels of exposure, these so-called endocrine-disrupting chemicals can alter sexual, neurological, and behavioral development, impair reproduction, and undermine immune systems. It's not merely a question of dying young; research suggests that some of these chemicals could leave generations of people with subtly impaired intellectual functioning, reduced fertility, and weakened immune systems.

"No one would have believed ten years ago what we're finding out today," said John Peterson Myers, a zoologist and co-author of *Our Stolen Future.* "Low doses matter. We're now aware that it doesn't take a lot to cause a big effect. The atrazine story is a case in point."

A research study published in the April 16 issue of *Proceedings of the National Academy of Sciences* found that exposure to as little as 0.1 parts per billion of atrazine, the most common weed killer in America, caused reproductive abnormalities in frogs.

Atrazine can be found everywhere—in rainwater, snow runoff, and groundwater. There is virtually no atrazine-free environment, according to Tyrone B. Hayes of the University of California, who led the research.

Regulating Pollutants

"We're in the midst of a revolution that started with Rachel Carson, and what we're learning today will require fundamental changes in how we structure regulating these chemicals," said Myers. "Faced with this kind of data, we can't keep looking at just one chemical at a time. We experience soups of chemicals that all interact with one another. There has to be a new standard—the system we have now is broken."

Change will not come easily or swiftly.

On April 12, the Bush administration announced that it was submitting the Stockholm Convention on Persistent Organic Pollutants (POPs) to Congress—with some modifications. The international treaty, approved by 127 nations in May 2001, calls for the complete elimination of the "Dirty Dozen": 12 chemicals that persist in the environment and are acknowledged to be extremely harmful to humans.

Although the United States signed the treaty, the enabling legislation sent to Congress eliminates a provision in the treaty that allows for the addition of new chemicals to the list if scientific evidence warrants it. Atrazine, the weed killer that causes frogs to develop male and female sex organs at concentrations 30 times lower than what is approved by the Environmental Protection Agency,* is not one of the 12 POPs named in the treaty.

The burden of proof in regulating chemicals needs to be changed from one in which harm must be demonstrated before a product is withdrawn, to an approach where safety is ensured beyond reasonable doubt before widespread deployment is allowed, Myers argues.

"Europe is far ahead of the United States in adopting a precautionary approach on this issue," said Myers. "The Swedish Chemicals Policy Committee has developed a standard that says if it's persistent and bioaccumulative, you don't need to show toxicity—that's enough. And that's the direction we need to be heading in."

Check Your Understanding

Check (✓) the statements that are *not* true, according to the two articles.

1. According to John Myers, the United States is more advanced than Europe in regulating chemicals.
2. Atrazine is a weed killer.
3. *Bioaccumulative* means substances that are toxic.
4. Insecticides before the war were mostly made of minerals and plants.
5. Insects were used in testing biochemical war weapons.
6. Low doses of toxic substances aren't a large concern to scientists.
7. Many people thought Rachel Carson was not a competent scientist.
8. Most synthetic insecticides were developed before World War II.
9. Pesticides build up in the bodies of living beings.
10. Pesticides occur nearly everywhere.

* The Environmental Protection Agency, or EPA, is an agency within the U.S. government.

11. Synthetic pesticides alter the way the body functions.
12. The "Dirty Dozen" refers to 12 harmful toxins.
13. *Time* magazine both criticized and praised Carson.
14. Tobacco is a synthetic pesticide.
15. Toxic poisons are often found in soup.

Group Discussion

Talk about these questions with your group or a partner.

1. According to the second reading, are pesticides more or less dangerous than they were in Rachel Carson's time?
2. Why do you think so many people criticized Carson for writing *Silent Spring?* Were they right to criticize her? Defend your answer.
3. Are you concerned about chemicals in the environment? Why or why not?
4. Insects are often harmful to people or plants. What can be done to control insects without harming the environment, in your opinion?

Language Focus: Preposition Practice

The following prepositional phrases are found in the reading. Choose the right preposition to fit into each sentence. In some cases, more than one answer is possible.

to from in about on by with at

1. Humans are often subjected _______ dangerous chemicals.
2. Toxins have been recovered _______ plants and animals.
3. Residues of pesticides linger _______ soil for many years.
4. Chemicals become lodged _______ the bodies of animals and plants.

5. Humans who are free ________ chemical exposure are nonexistent.
6. Many animals burrow ________ the soil.
7. The poisoning of the soil came ________ because of synthetic pesticides.
8. ________ the course of developing chemical weapons, scientists discovered insecticides.
9. The discovery did not come ________ chance, as a matter of fact.
10. Humans have waged chemical warfare ________ the environment.
11. The forests were teeming ________ animals.
12. The illness was brought ________ by people using chemicals.
13. Even ________ low levels of exposure, chemicals can be dangerous.
14. The atrazine story is a case ________ point.
15. We cannot study just one chemical ________ a time.

Chapter Wrap-Up

Speaking Activities

Class Reports

1. Meet with students who read the same reading you did. Review the questions at the end of the reading.
2. Think of one question to ask your group about the reading. Take turns asking your questions.
3. Choose someone from your group to give a report to the class. In your report, tell your classmates what you learned from your reading.
4. Find a site on the Internet about the environment. Two examples are The National Geographic Society, *www.nationalgeographic.com,*

and The World Wildlife Fund, *www.worldwildlife.org*. Describe to members of the other groups what you discovered on the site you looked at.

5. Teach students in other groups one important word you learned from this chapter.

Discussion

1. What does it mean to be a hero?
2. Do you do anything to help the environment? Why or why not? What do you do?
3. Who should take care of the environment, the world's governments or individual citizens? Explain your answer.
4. In your community, what activities should be done to help the local environment? How can local community members become involved?

Writing Ideas

Write one or two paragraphs describing your favorite outdoor place to visit. Is there water? A beach? A forest? Include a lot of details.

Do you enjoy eating fish? Have you ever been fishing? Are you worried about overfishing and the environment? Write a page about fish, fishing, or overfishing.

Is pollution a problem in your local community or your home country? Describe the problem and propose a solution in a short essay (three or four paragraphs).

If you could dive under the sea, or travel across the ocean to see wildlife, would you go? If not, what adventures would you like to have?

For Your Journal

Who is your hero? Why is that person heroic to you? What has he or she done that is special in your opinion?

APPENDIX

1 Suggested Videos

Chapter 1. Introduction: Study Skills

Spellbound (2002). This documentary follows eight teenagers on their quest to win the 1999 U.S. National Spelling Bee.

Finding Forrester (2000). An American teenager is an excellent writer and finds a famous but secretive author to be his mentor.

Chapter 2. Communication: Language and Culture

Lost in Translation (2003). Two Americans in Tokyo feel the difficulty of culture shock and become friends.

Rabbit-Proof Fence (2002). In 1931, three aboriginal girls escape after being taken from their homes to be trained as domestic staff. They walk across the Australian Outback.

Chapter 3. Education: Genius

A Beautiful Mind (2001). A brilliant mathematician overcomes mental illness and receives the Nobel Prize.

The Miracle Worker (1962). The story of Anne Sullivan's struggle to teach the blind and deaf Helen Keller how to communicate.

Chapter 4. English: American Short Stories

Fahrenheit 451 (1966). Ray Bradbury's story about censorship and book burning.

The Human Comedy (1943). The story of small town life during World War II, written by William Saroyan.

Chapter 5. Art: Art of the Americas

Magic in the Sky (1981). This movie looks at the effect of television on the Inuit people of the Canadian Arctic. The film also shows the start of the first Inuit-language television network, called Inukshuk.

Frida (2002). The story of the life of the Mexican artist Frida Kahlo.

Chapter 6. History: Slavery

Amistad (1997). The story of the Amistad slave-ship rebellion.

Roots (1977). A television mini-series following the author Alex Haley's family line from ancestor Kunta Kinte's enslavement to his descendents' liberation.

Chapter 7. Business: Business Communication

Working Girl (1988). A secretary works for a difficult boss and learns to have confidence in her own work.

Office Space (1999). A comedy about office workers who hate their jobs and decide to rebel against their greedy boss.

Chapter 8. Geology: The Earth's Fury

Twister (1996). A couple considering divorce keep meeting each other because both are researchers who chase tornadoes.

Dante's Peak (1997). Dr. Harry Dalton discovers that Dante's Peak, a favorite place to live in America, is being threatened by a volcano.

Chapter 9. Nutrition: Kitchen Science

Big Night (1996). Two brothers run a failing Italian restaurant. One night they take a risk to try to save the business.

Tortilla Soup (2001). A Mexican-American chef and father of three daughters loses his taste for food.

Chapter 10. Ecology: Heroes of the Environment

Whale Rider (2003). A story of a young Maori girl who fights to fulfill a destiny her grandfather refuses to recognize.

The Day after Tomorrow (2004). A climatologist tries to find a way to save the world from sudden global warming.

APPENDIX

2 Extended Reading Suggestions

Reading outside of class, especially whole books, will help your English skills. Books that are particularly good for lower-level students are marked with an asterisk.

Chapter 1. Introduction: Study Skills

What Smart Students Know: Maximum Grades. Optimum Learning. Minimum Time by Adam Robinson
Write to Learn by Donald Morison Murray

Chapter 2. Communication: Language and Culture

Iron and Silk by Mark Salzman
Language, Culture, and Communication: The Meaning of Messages (4th Edition) by Nancy Bonvillain

Chapter 3. Education: Genius

Autobiography of Malcolm X by Malcolm X
The Story of My Life by Helen Keller*

Chapter 4. English: American Short Stories

The Martian Chronicles by Ray Bradbury
The William Saroyan Reader by William Saroyan*

Chapter 5. Art: Art of the Americas

Between the Lines: The Mystery of the Giant Ground Drawings of Ancient Nasca, Peru by Anthony F. Aveni
My Art, My Life: An Autobiography by Diego Rivera

Chapter 6. History: Slavery

Beloved by Toni Morrison
Slaves in the Family by Edward Ball

Chapter 7. Business: Business Communication

How to Win Friends and Influence People by Dale Carnegie
What's Your Point? The 3-Step Method for Making Effective Presentations by Bob Boylan

Chapter 8. Geology: The Earth's Fury

Eyewitness: Hurricane and Tornado by Jack Challoner*
Krakatoa by Simon Winchester

Chapter 9. Nutrition: Kitchen Science

Fast Food Nation by Eric Schlosser
How to Read a French Fry by Russ Parsons

Chapter 10. Ecology: Heroes of the Environment

Jacques Cousteau: Saving Our Seas by Lorraine Jean Hopping*
Silent Spring by Rachel Carson

APPENDIX

3 Related Websites

There is a lot of information available on the Internet. However, sometimes Internet addresses change, so the following information may become out of date.

Chapter 1. Introduction: Study Skills

Purdue University's Online Writing Lab: *http://owl.english.purdue.edu*
The Great Books Foundation: *http://www.greatbooks.org*

Chapter 2. Communication: Language and Culture

PBS, The New Americans: *http://www.pbs.org/independentlens/newamericans/*
Word Origins: *http://www.wordorigins.org*

Chapter 3. Education: Genius

PBS, Nova, Secrets of the Mind: *http://www.pbs.org/wgbh/nova/mind/*
Wired Magazine, The Key to Genius: *http://www.wired.com/wired/archive/11.12/genius_pr.html*

Chapter 4. English: American Short Stories

Classic Reader: *http://www.classicreader.com*
Zoetrope All Story: *http://www.all-story.com*

Chapter 5. Art: Art of the Americas

Inuit Art: *http://collections.ic.gc.ca/cape_dorset/*
The Great Wall of Los Angeles: *http://www.sparcmurals.org/product/greatwall/greatwallmain.html*

Chapter 6. History: Slavery

Born in Slavery: *http://memory.loc.gov/ammem/snhtml/snhome.html*
American Anti-Slavery Group: *http://www.iabolish.com/b2/*

Chapter 7. Business: Business Communication

Job Web: *http://www.jobweb.com*
Business 2.0 Magazine: *http://www.business2.com*

Chapter 8. Geology: The Earth's Fury

PBS, Hunt for the Supertwister: *http://www.pbs.org/wgbh/nova/tornado/*
U.S. Geological Survey Earthquake Site: *http://quake.wr.usgs.gov*

Chapter 9. Nutrition: Kitchen Science

Food & Nutrition Information Center: *http://www.nal.usda.gov/fnic/*
Food TV: *http://www.foodtv.com*

Chapter 10. Ecology: Heroes of the Environment

Cousteau Society: *http://www.cousteau.org*
U.S. Environmental Protection Agency: *http://www.epa.gov*

APPENDIX

4 Vocabulary Practiced by Level

The chapter(s) in which each word or collocation is introduced and practiced is given in parentheses.

First Step

abolitionist (6)
apparatus (10)
applaud (4)
attitude (2)
attract (4)
beard (5)
body language (2)
captor (6)
caribou (5)
cereal (9)
clean-shaven (4)
collide (8)
communication (2)
conductor (4)
confuse (3)
container (9)
convenient (1)
coral reef (10)
cucumber (9)
current (6)
customer (7)
detect (8)
direct (7)
disconnect (7)
district (4)
diver (10)
dolphin (10)
drown out (4)
envy (4)
etiquette (7)
exactly (4)
expect (4)
fable (4)
facial expression (2)
finance (10)
frown (2)
frustrating (7)
gesture (2)
hail (8)
hatch (5)
hazy (5)
heartbroken (6)
imitate (3)
impression (7)
indication (5)
inland (5)
interrupt (1)
kidnap (6)
leafy (9)
lightning (8)
mass (8)
minerals (9)
moisture (8)
motion (3)
mug (3)
mystery (3)
opposite (4)
organize (1)

piracy (6)
planner (1)
plantation (6)
posture (2)
pressure (8)
pretext (4)
proud (3)
rebel (6)
refresh (1) (5)
respect (1)
résumé (7)
secure (5)
severe (8)
shelter (8)
shrink (10)
sincere (2)
slightly (4)
solemn (4)
spout (3)
stare (4)
steer (6)
swept (3)
thigh (5)
tornado (8)
transport (5)
underwater (10)
vacate (4)
vegetarian (9)
violation (6)
vitamins (9)
voicemail (7)
walrus (5)
warning (4)
wrinkle (4)

Second Step

acidity (9)
affiliation (7)
anchor (10)
aqueduct (5)
artichoke (9)
ascendancy (10)
assimilate (1)
brittle (4)
bullet point (7)
canal (4)
cataclysm (8)
chard (9)
chronological (7)
clarify (1)
comb (10)
comeback (2)
cove (10)
credibility (8)
crisscross (5)
cutlery (4)
daunting (3)
decree (2)
depleted (10)
designate (8)
dredging (10)
edible (9)
emphatically (9)
erode (4)
fervently (4)
fleet (10)
fluke (8)
forecast (8)
gaze (4)
geophysicist (8)
gloom (10)
grab (6)
gravel (5)
grub (6)
haunt (2) (3)
heritage (2)
hoarsely (4)

holocaust (2)
hospitable (10)
humidity (10)
ideologies (10)
indulge (3)
irreparably (9)
keywords (1)
linen (4)
linoleum (4)
lure (4)
magnitude (8)
major (7)
minor (7)
mirage (10)
nomination (3)
non-controversial (7)
observatory (5)
omit (1)
optional (7)
outdated (7)
pagan (2)
parallel (5)
parch (4)
pension (6)
platter (4)
podium (3)
potential (7)
powwow (2)
probability (8)
prodigal (10)
provisions (6)
purification (2)
qualification (8)
ramifications (10)
reinforce (1)
résumé (7)
revamp (8)
rhubarb (9)
sapling (2)
scar (6)
schizophrenia (3)
scholar (3)
scorch (4)
shrine (5)
slits (4)
squawk (3)
stun (3)
substantial (3)
subterranean (9)
tarmac (5)
tattered (1)
technique (1)
tenant (4)
timber (10)
trapezoid (5)
traumatic (2)
unreprimanded (4)
vague (9)
volunteer (7)
wringing (4)

Third Step

aardvark (3)
abject (2)
acrimony (9)
aftermath (8)
alfalfa (4)
anarchist (5)
assimilate (7)
avert (2)
baleful (2)
balk (5)
banquet (9)
beholder (5)
bioaccumulative (10)
biochemistry (1)
biodiversity (10)

blight (2)
bouillon (9)
brazenly (2)
buffet (2)
bug (7)
burrow (3) (10)
cannibalism (1)
capricious (4)
caricature (5)
coed (2)
compression (1)
concise (1)
contamination (10)
contemplate (6)
convalescence (5)
corporate ladder (7)
culminate (8)
culpable (6)
defunct (5)
deluge (8)
depiction (5)
deployment (10)
detonation (8)
dire (9)
emancipation (5)
emulate (3)
endocrine (10)
entrepreneur (9)
eruption (8)
eventually (6)
exemplification (5)
extension (7)
fathom (2)
ferocity (8)
finally (6)
fresco (5)
furor (5)
gastronomic (9)
grove (2)
hearty (4)
herbicide (10)
hone (6)
inanimate (10)
inaudibly (8)
inevitable (1)
insecticidal (10)
intangible (6)
intransigent (5)
inundate (8)
latter-day (6)
lauded (9)
leftist (5)
legacy (6)
leguminous (10)
live on (6)
longing (4)
magnificence (4)
malignancy (10)
marquee (5)
marquis (5)
memorial (2)
monograph (1)
mortify (2)
mulled (9)
mural (5)
nightingale (2)
nuance (7)
oblige (5)
oust (5)
oxidation (10)
pagoda (2)
painstaking (3)
panacea (9)
pedigreed (6)
penmanship (3)
periphery (9)
pesticide (10)
pious (4)

prewar (10)
prodigious (10)
progeny (6)
proletariat (5)
psychoanalysis (6)
pumice (8)
pun (1)
puree (9)
quintessence (9)
residue (10)
résumé (7)
riffling (3)
scaffold (5)
shaft (5)
shrine (2)
sinister (10)
spew (2)
standings (1)
stellar (7)
strait (8)
surrealist (5)
surrey (4)
swelter (2)
swooping (1)
synergistic (10)
tableau (5)
taboo (6)
teem (10)
termites (3)
transgression (2)
ubiquitous (9)
unbridled (8)
usually (6)
validity (10)
vigor (8)
wail (2)
well-heeled (9)
wreath (5)
xenophobic (7)
zoologist (10)

Answer Key

1. Introduction

First Step

Vocabulary (page 2)

1. a
2. b
3. c
4. a
5. c

Check Your Understanding (page 4)

1. b
2. c
3. a

Language Focus: Idioms (page 4)

take a break: take some time off from studying
keep the music low: keep the music quiet or turned down
keep to a schedule: plan when to do your work, and do it at that time
get right to work: start working now

1. keep the music low
2. get right to work
3. keep to a schedule
4. take a break
5. get right to work

Second Step

Vocabulary (page 6)

technique: a method or practice of doing something
omit: to leave something out
keyword: a word that carries the main idea
clarify: to make something clear
reinforce: to make something stronger
assimilate: to blend or mix into something

Check Your Understanding (page 9)

1. false
2. true
3. true
4. false
5. true
6. false
7. false

Language Focus: Preposition Practice (page 10)

1. into, on, on
2. in, on, of
3. to
4. in
5. blank, to
6. at, of
7. blank, from
8. by
9. on, on, of
10. for, of
11. There are different ways to answer this question, but one possibility is: Draw a red heart in the corner of the box. Put it in the top left corner.

Third Step

Vocabulary (page 12)

1. standings: position or status
2. swooping: diving or plunging
3. inevitable: unavoidable
4. monographs: long pieces of academic writing about a specific subject.
5. pun: a play on words
6. cannibalism: the practice of humans eating human flesh, or the complete eating of something
7. bog down in: to become stuck in something, to slow down one's progress
8. concise: short and to the point
9. compression: the squeezing of something to make it a smaller size

Sample sentences will vary.

Check Your Understanding (page 22)

1. d
2. e
3. c
4. b
5. e.
6. a
7. c
8. d

Language Focus: Metaphors (page 24)

1. stores or supplies
   Just as a grocer stocks the shelves in a supermarket, reading supplies information into our minds.
2. carries
   Although one doesn't really "wear" his or her fears like a badge, we carry them on ourselves, and others might see them.
3. open
   Although you don't use a key to unlock meaning like a key opens a door, clues help us to open the meaning of a book.
4. land
   Although a book isn't a piece of land or property, just as we walk through a territory, we travel through the pages of a book.
5. knitted together
   Just as you might weave a green thread into a sweater, you can weave, or knit, a meaning into a text.
6. Answers will vary.

2. Communication

Icebreaker (page 28)

1. They are in a classroom.
2. The woman wants to ask a question or speak in class. She is raising her hand to show the teacher this.
3. The man is listening, or paying attention. He may be taking notes.
4. Answers may vary.

First Step

Vocabulary (page 29)

1. b
2. e
3. f
4. c
5. g
6. a
7. d

Check Your Understanding (page 31)

1. c
2. b
3. a
4. d
5. c
6. d

Language Focus: by + doing (page 32)

1. by smiling
2. by using
3. by frowning
4. by speaking
5. by wearing
6. Answers will vary.

Second Step

Vocabulary (page 33)

1. heritage: tradition or custom
2. comeback: fast answer
3. decree: an announcement
4. holocaust: terrible destruction
5. purification: making something clean and pure
6. pagan: a person who has no religion
7. sapling: young tree
8. haunt: to appear, as a ghost does
9. traumatic: upsetting, troubling
10. powwow: a Native American or First Nations gathering and celebration

Check Your Understanding (page 36)

1. The Ojibwa are a group of Native Americans in the northern U.S. and Canada.
2. Answers will vary.
3. Canadian residential schools were places where young Indians were sent to live away from their families. They learned to be servants there.

4. The residential schools harmed Ojibwa families.
5. Many of the older people and family members did not learn their culture at residential schools, so it is hard for them to pass it along.

Language Focus: Specialized Vocabulary (page 37)
Answers will vary.

Third Step

Vocabulary (page 38)
memorial: monument
pagoda: a Japanese temple
Shinto shrine: Shinto is a Japanese religion; a shrine is a type of religious monument
bamboo grove: bamboo is a type of plant; a grove is a group of plants growing together
nightingale: a bird known for its singing
fathom: to understand
corps de ballet: group of ballet dancers
brazenly: boldly
swelter: to be too hot
coed: a female student (short for "co-educational")
avert: to turn away
mortify: to embarrass deeply
transgression: a mistake
spew: spit out
wail: cry or howl
blight: stain or scar
baleful: sad or pitiful
terra cognita: Latin for "known territory"
abject: complete
buffet: to toss around

Check Your Understanding (page 44)
1. She was invited to go.
2. She didn't understand the cultural differences.
3. She liked the culture and had respect for it.
4. She crossed her arms when she listened to people, which means that one is bored.
5. Kingsolver was sad and moved by the monument. She saw the monument as a symbol of the Japanese forgiveness for the atomic bomb that was dropped on Hiroshima.
6. Answers will vary, but in general Kingsolver is feeling grateful that she is beginning to understand Japanese culture, and what she believes is a "culture of forgiveness."

Language Focus: Idioms (page 45)
1. I like to look and act like the people around me when I travel.
2. I asked many different people to find out more about Japan.
3. I was approximately 8 inches taller (the height of a head) than all the other passengers.
4. I couldn't understand the process of showering with a hand-held nozzle.
5. I crossed my arms when I listened, which is the sign for showing boredom.
6. And so it happened that I arrived in Kyoto an utter foreigner, unprepared.
7. Answers will vary.

3. Education

First Step

Vocabulary (page 50)
1. f
2. h
3. d
4. e
5. b
6. a
7. c
8. g

Check Your Understanding (page 53)
1. false
2. false
3. true
4. false
5. true

Language Focus: Preposition Practice (page 54)

1. of
2. on
3. for
4. in
5. of
6. in
7. in
8. on
9. to
10. for

Second Step

Vocabulary (page 55)

schizophrenia: a type of mental illness
scholar: a serious student
daunting: frightening, intimidating
haunt: trouble, disturb
stunned: quietly and greatly surprised
nominations: recommendations, proposals
substantial: large
podium: a type of platform where speakers stand to give speeches
squawk: a noise, like that made by a chicken
indulge: treat, give into

Check Your Understanding (page 58)

1. c
2. b
3. d
4. c
5. a
6. d
7. b

Language Focus: Sentence Fragments (page 60)

Answers will vary. Examples given below.

1. Maybe you can teach in the spring.
2. Hey Nash, are you scared?
3. You came to see if I'd screw everything up if I actually won.
4. You are worried that maybe I'll dance at the podium or strip naked and squawk like a chicken.
5. It's like a diet of the mind.
6. I do not indulge my appetite for patterns, and perhaps my appetite to imagine, even to dream.

Third Step

Vocabulary (page 61)

1. emulate: imitate
2. penmanship: style of handwriting
3. riffling: thumbing through (the pages of a book, for example)
4. painstaking: careful
5. burrowing: digging into
6. termites: types of insects that eat wood

Example sentences will vary.

Check Your Understanding (page 64)

1. Eighth grade.
2. He seemed to be reading, but he didn't really understand the words or sentences.
3. The dictionary was very important to him. It taught him about the words of English, their meanings, and how to write them.
4. Education and learning to read had made him free, even though he was in prison.

Language Focus: Understanding Complex Sentences (page 65)

Answers will vary. Examples given.

1. It had really begun back in the Charlestown Prison, when Bimbi first made me envious of how much he knew.
2. In my slow, careful, sloppy handwriting, I copied into my tablet everything printed on that first page, including the punctuation marks.
3. It's funny, from the dictionary's first page right now, I remember the word "aardvark."
4. With each page that followed, I also learned of people and places and events from history.

5. I think it was normal that as I learned more words, I could for the first time pick up a book and read and now begin to understand what the book was saying.
6. It would have been impossible to make me stop reading.

4. English

Icebreaker (page 68)

1. "The Tortoise and the Hare." The story tells of a race between a tortoise and a rabbit (hare). Although the rabbit is faster, the tortoise wins the race because he continues to walk, while the rabbit plays and relaxes.
2. Answers will vary.
3. Answers will vary.

First Step

Vocabulary (page 69)

fable: tale or story
clean-shaven: freshly shaved, without a beard or mustache
slightly: a little
exactly: precisely
envying: being jealous of, wishing one had the same things as someone else
attracted: drawn to
staring: looking at without stopping
district: area
opposite: across from
pretext: reason, excuse
vacated: left empty
warning: caution or advice
drowned out: hard to hear
wrinkled: rumpled, not smooth
applauded: clapped, congratulated
expected: waited for
conductor: person who collects tickets on a train
solemn: serious

Check Your Understanding (page 75)

a. 5
b. 3
c. 6
d. 10
e. 8
f. 7
g. 9
h. 12
i. 11
j. 2
k. 1
l. 4

Language Focus: Two-Word Verbs (page 76)

1. drowned out
2. work your way up
3. gets off
4. start up
5. get on
6. started up
7. drown out
8. get off

Second Step

Vocabulary (page 76)

tenant: renter
linoleum: type of floor covering
unreprimanded: not scolded
slits: small openings
lured: enticed
gazed: looked at
linen: type of cloth
platter: large plate
hoarsely: with a raspy voice
cutlery: eating utensils, such as a knife and fork
brittle: breakable
canal: a narrow waterway
eroded: worn away
scorched: burned
parched: hot and dry
fervently: with great eagerness
wringing: twisting

Check Your Understanding (page 82)

1. c
2. b
3. a
4. c
5. b

Language Focus: Adjective Order (page 83)

Answers will vary.

Third Step

Vocabulary (page 84)

1. magnificence: grandness
2. longing: wanting, yearning
3. pious: serious, religious
4. capricious: unpredictable, unreliable
5. alfalfa: a type of grass fed to animals
6. hearty: large, filling
7. surrey: type of carriage

Sample sentences will vary.

Check Your Understanding (page 93)

1. Aram
2. Mourad
3. John Byro
4. the San Joaquin Valley
5. Armenian
6. Uncle Khosrove
7. Zorab
8. nine
9. honesty
10. My Heart

Language Focus: Idioms (page 94)

1. dawned on
2. For all anybody knew
3. no question about it.
4. For the sake of
5. had a way with
6. let alone
7. crazy about
8. the old country
9. no matter what
10. On the one hand

5. Art

First Step

Vocabulary (page 98)

1. c
2. d
3. h
4. i
5. a
6. e
7. b
8. j
9. g
10. j

Check Your Understanding (page 101)

1. b
2. c
3. a
4. c
5. b
6. a

Language Focus: Animal Names (page 102)
Answers will vary. Example answers:

1. walrus: This large animal has big teeth. It lives in the water. It looks black, and has large whiskers on its face.
2. caribou: A large reindeer. It has brown fur and long thin legs.
3. seal: This animal lives in the water. It has short black fur. It's very fat and sleek, and has small flippers and very small ears.
4. bird: This animal flies and has feathers. There are lots of different sizes and colors of birds.

Answers 5 through 10 will vary.

Second Step

Vocabulary (page 103)

1. parallel: two lines that are the same distance apart, like this: | |
2. trapezoid: a four-sided figure with two sides that are parallel, like this: 
3. crisscross: a pattern of lines that crosses over each other
4. gravel: small stones
5. tarmac: material used on the surface of roads, or the surface of an area where planes land
6. observatory: a place for watching stars, usually through telescopes
7. shrine: a religious holy place where people worship
8. aqueduct: a pipe or canal for moving water across a long distance

Sample sentences will vary.

Check Your Understanding (page 107)

1. Peru
2. biomorphs and geoglyphs
3. biomorphs
4. An airplane pilot spotted them from above.
5. He thought the lines had been created so that visitors from outer space could land their spaceships.
6. He thought that the lines were astronomically significant—that the plain was like a huge space observatory.
7. religious shrines
8. They believe that the shapes on the Nasca plain may make up a large map of underground water sources.
9. because they are so large

Language Focus: Names of Shapes (page 108)

1. parallel lines	
2. intersecting lines	
3. trapezoid	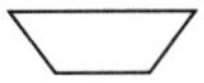
4. spiral	
5. triangle	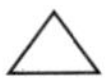

Third Step

Vocabulary (page 109)

leftist: someone with left-wing (liberal) beliefs
oust: kick out
oblige: require
convalescence: period of healing
surrealist: an artist of an early 20th-century artistic movement that tried to represent the subconscious by creating fantastic and dream-like images
beholder: one who sees
shaft: a long, slender handle
exemplification: illustration
mural: large painting done on a wall
fresco: a type of painting on plaster
caricature: a cartoon drawing that exaggerates someone's features
depiction: a picture or description of something
defunct: outdated, no longer working
intransigent: firmly or stubbornly refusing to change one's mind
tableau: a visually exciting scene or situation, a painting
balk: to stop suddenly and refuse to go on, to resist something
emancipation: freedom
scaffold: a framework or structure
furor: excitement, often anger
proletariat: the class of wage-earning workers in a society
marquee: a sign over a theater
marquis: a type of European nobleman
anarchists: people who reject the need for an organized government
lie in state: when dead, to have one's body exhibited publicly
wreath: a ring of flowers or greenery

Check Your Understanding (page 115)

1. B
2. B
3. K
4. R
5. K
6. K
7. R
8. R
9. blank
10. R
11. R
12. blank
13. R
14. K
15. blank

Language Focus: Understanding Complex Language (page 116)
Answers will vary. Examples given.

1. She made her last public appearance in a wheelchair at a meeting here to support the government of

Communist-supported President Jacobo Arbenz Guzman of Guatemala, which has now been removed.
2. Frida Kahlo began painting in 1926 while doctors made her stay in bed while she recovered from injuries suffered in a bus accident.
3. Consistently radical in his painting and writing, and totally controversial his whole lifetime (at least from the age of 5, according to one story), Diego Rivera was the best example of an artistic rebirth in his native Mexico.
4. Physically huge, grand in his ideas and how he carried them out, Señor Rivera practiced in art's biggest hall, painting large wall frescoes that celebrated the world's workers and cruelly made fun of persons of authority and wealth.
5. Some people criticized his beliefs harshly, but many famous artists and critics, who believed his murals were masterpieces, defended him just as strongly.
6. What might have become the most highly viewed painting, a mural in the main building of Rockefeller Center, was turned into dust and small pieces of plaster and removed after the stubborn painter decided to make Nikolai Lenin the main figure of a huge painting, representing him as mankind's leader.
7. He told people who believed in Communist ideals who supported him that he painted in the United States not merely as an artist but also to support the average working person.
8. It began when Miss Kahlo's coffin was covered in the Soviet Union flag while it was displayed in public in the National Institute of Fine Arts in Mexico City.

6. History

First Step

Vocabulary (page 121)
Answers will vary.

Check Your Understanding (page 124)
1. b
2. c
3. d
4. a
5. d

Language Focus: Preposition Practice (page 125)
1. d
2. c
3. b
4. a
5. b
6. d
7. c
8. b

Second Step

Vocabulary (page 127)
1. f
2. c
3. b
4. a
5. g
6. d
7. e

Check Your Understanding (page 129)
1. true
2. true
3. false
4. false
5. true
6. true
7. true
8. false
9. true
10. false

Language Focus: Spoken and Written Language (page 130)
1. My owners were Robert and Mary Ball.
2. They had four children that I knew.
3. Some of them ran off.
4. Bob Ball didn't use any dogs.

5. I ran away to Louisville to join the Yankees one day.
6. They said they were fighting for us—for our freedom.
7. My folks were still at my master's.
8. They hadn't raised anything to eat the last two years.
9. I've been here in Forrest City twenty or more years.
10. They're going to send me a ticket and pay all my expenses.

Third Step

Vocabulary (page 131)

1. hone: to sharpen something
2. taboo: forbidden, not allowed
3. contemplate: consider, think about
4. psychoanalysis: a method of analyzing the events of someone's life to discover the problems and their sources
5. latter-day: resembling a person from the past
6. intangible: difficult to define or describe, without any substance
7. pedigreed: having a document showing the line of ancestors
8. culpable: guilty
9. legacy: something that is left from a previous generation
10. progeny: offspring, heirs

Sample sentences will vary.

Check Your Understanding (page 135)

1. The side of the British, who eventually lost to the Americans.
2. The Americans took them after the British lost the war.
3. Although it was history, and a serious history of slaves, it was a type of family story that might be told to children. In other words, it did not contain any details that would not be suitable for children to hear.
4. His ancestors' opinion, but not his own. He does not think that slaves were "half human."
5. He feels proud of the stories about his family, and sentimental about his ancestors and family members.
6. He states that he does not feel guilty, but that he feels responsible to explain what happened.
7. The plantations live on because they are part of the history of the people still living today.

Language Focus: Time Words and Phrases (page 137)

Answers will vary.

7. Business

First Step

Vocabulary (page 141)

1. direct
2. etiquette
3. voicemail
4. impression
5. frustrating
6. on hold
7. disconnected
8. customer

Check Your Understanding (page 144)

1. Your name and the reason you are calling.
2. Use a phrase like, "Good Afternoon," and then state your name and your company's name. Ask how you can help the caller.
3. Message pads and pens or pencils.
4. Give the caller a choice, by saying, "May I put you on hold or should I call you back?"
5. impression
6. Speak clearly and spell your name. Speak all numbers slowly, especially if you are using voicemail. If you leave a long message, state your name and phone number again at the end of the message. Always say why you are calling.
7. On the first or second ring.

Language Focus: Understanding Etiquette (page 145)
Answers will vary.

Second Step

Vocabulary (page 146)
1. c
2. f
3. h
4. e
5. d
6. b
7. i
8. a
9. g

Check Your Understanding (page 150)
1. b
2. c
3. b
4. d
5. a
6. c

Language Focus: Preposition Practice (page 152)
1. In
2. to
3. by
4. in
5. in, in
6. for
7. at
8. with or at
9. to
10. in

Third Step

Vocabulary (page 153)
1. stellar: very good
2. assimilate: blend into
3. corporate ladder: the structure or hierarchy of the corporation. One speaks of "moving up the corporate ladder" as a way of talking about promotion and advancement.
4. university extension: an organization attached to a public university which does not require (usually) application or admission. Anyone in the community may pay to take classes there.
5. nuance: hint
6. bug (slang, verb): bother
7. xenophobic: afraid of foreigners
8. grounds for: reasons for

Sample sentences will vary.

Check Your Understanding (page 155)
1. d
2. b
3. c
4. a
5. d

Language Focus: Idioms (page 157)
Answers will vary.

8. Geology

First Step

Vocabulary (page 161)
1. tornado: a funnel-shaped rotating cloud that is very damaging
2. severe: extreme, strong
3. moisture: wetness, dampness
4. pressure: a force of air or water
5. mass: a body
6. collide: to hit something
7. lightning: flashes of light in the sky caused by storms
8. hail: frozen rain
9. detect: notice or discover
10. shelter: something that covers people or other things

Check Your Understanding (page 164)
1. b
2. a
3. b
4. c
5. d
6. b
7. c

Language Focus: Size and Number (page 166)

1. The wind was blowing 20 mile per hour. miles per hour
2. Tornadoes can be over 400 foot wide. feet
3. A tornado usually lasts just a few minute. minutes
4. A supercell is severals miles wide. several
5. There were over a thousands tornadoes in the U.S. in 2003. thousand
6. VORTEX started in 1994. In 2004, it was a ten-years-old project. ten-year-old
7. Tornadoes can spin over 110 mphs. mph

Second Step

Vocabulary (page 167)

1. cataclysm
2. fluke
3. forecast
4. bull's-eye
5. credibility
6. magnitude
7. qualification
8. probability
9. revamp
10. designate

Check Your Understanding (page 169)

1. March 2003.
2. A 60 percent probability of an 8.1 magnitude quake in the vicinity of Japan's Tokachi Plain on the island of Hokkaido over the next 30 years.
3. A 100-by-150-mile area just offshore from the Tokachi Plain.
4. The government formed the committee after the 1995 earthquake in Kobe, Japan, partly to renew that nation's effort to forecast and plan for future quakes.
5. He thinks it might just be a coincidence that they forecast this one. They need to forecast more earthquakes before he believes they are completely successful.

Language Focus: Phrases of Time and Location (page 170)

Answers will vary.

Third Step

Vocabulary (page 171)

eruption: the violent release of gas, steam, ash, or lava from a volcano
vigor: strength
deluge: flood
pumice: a very light type of stone
unbridled: without any restrictions or things to slow it down
ferocity: strength
inaudibly: silently
detonation: explosion, blowing up of something
culminate: result
strait: a narrow body of water that connects two larger bodies
inundate: flood, overwhelm
aftermath: consequences of a disastrous event

Check Your Understanding (page 174)

Answers will vary. Examples given.

8 p.m. Volcanic energy traveled through the water, and the Sunda strait became very unsettled.
11:32 p.m. Because of the volcanic vibrations, the time ball on the harbor's clock stopped.
Just before midnight: Explosions could be heard, even as far as Singapore and Penang.
1:55 a.m. The gas lanterns dimmed along the main shopping street, and several windows shattered.
4 a.m. The explosions became less continuous but more explosive.
4:56 a.m. A huge air wave was felt at the Batavia gasworks.
5:30 a.m. The first gigantic explosion happened.
6:15 a.m. Ketimbang, Sumatra, was destroyed.

6:44 a.m. The second large explosion happened.
10:02 a.m. The final, largest explosion occurred.

Language Focus: Understanding Complex Language (page 175)
Answers will vary. Examples given.

1. By 8 p.m. volcanic energy was traveling through the water, and as night came the sea in the Sunda Strait became fierce and agitated.
2. The sound of the explosions began to travel outward too, and there was a report from Singapore and Penang that thudding sounds could be heard at about the same time.
3. The final explosion—though no one on the ground at the time knew it—was soon to happen.
4. The Sumatran town of Ketimbang was then destroyed at 6:15 a.m., and Anjer, its Javan sister port across the water—according to the few who survived to tell about it—was flooded and wrecked very shortly afterwards.
5. After Krakatoa's eruption, 165 villages were ruined, 36,417 people died, and many thousands were injured—almost all of them, villages and villagers, were not victims of the eruption directly but of the huge sea-waves that were sent from the volcano during the last night of explosions.

9. Nutrition

First Step

Vocabulary (page 179)
1. vegetarian
2. container
3. cucumber
4. cereal
5. leafy
6. vitamins, minerals

Check Your Understanding (page 181)
1. d
2. c
3. b
4. c
5. d

Language Focus: Fruit and Vegetable Words (page 183)
Answers will vary. From the photo, there are: cabbage, onions, peppers, strawberries, grapes, mushrooms, avacados, eggplant, tomatoes, bananas, squash

Second Step

Vocabulary (page 184)
Some answers may vary.

1. similar to a root
2. a green vegetable with leaves like a flower and a sharp part in the middle
3. a large green leafy vegetable
4. strongly
5. underground
6. a vegetable that looks like celery, but has red stalks
7. unclear
8. cannot be fixed
9. lemon, lime
10. peach, plum, cherry

Check Your Understanding (page 186)
1. true
2. false
3. false
4. true
5. false
6. true
7. true
8. false
9. true
10. true

Language Focus: Fruit and Vegetable Words (page 187)
Answers will vary.

Third Step

Vocabulary (page 189)
banquet: large feast
puree: to chop or blend food so it becomes a liquid

meat stock: a liquid that remains from boiling meat in water
mulled: warmed with spices
bouillon: a liquid made from boiling meat or vegetables with water
ubiquitous: everywhere
gruel: a thick grain soup
laud: congratulate
panacea: something that cures all ailments
acrimony: bitterness
dire: severe
periphery: edge
entrepreneur: someone who makes money through business opportunities
gastronomic: related to food and eating
quintessence: ideal
well-heeled: having a large income or a lot of property

Check Your Understanding (page 193)

1. A thick puree of rice and chicken moistened with milk from ground almonds, then sprinkled with sugar and fried pork fat.
2. A mulled red wine seasoned with ground ginger, cinnamon, cloves and sugar.
3. Thick purees, lots of spices, sweet and sour sauces, cooked vegetables, and warmed wines.
4. Sugar was ubiquitous as a seasoning in savory dishes.
5. It didn't change it much; except for turkey, the dishes didn't include many new ingredients.
6. On the one hand, most people can afford a Western diet, but it is not completely healthy, as it contains too much fat.
7. Restaurant means "healthy food" in this reading. This came as part of the development of medicine and its relationship to food.

Language Focus: Article Practice (page 194)

1. nothing
2. a or the
3. a or the
4. The or nothing
5. a
6. nothing
7. nothing
8. nothing
9. nothing
10. nothing
11. nothing
12. a
13. nothing
14. nothing
15. a
16. nothing
17. nothing
18. nothing
19. nothing

10. Ecology

First Step

Vocabulary (page 198)
Answers will vary.

Check Your Understanding (page 201)

a. 1
b. 6
c. 10
d. 5
e. 2
f. 9
g. 4
h. 7
i. 8
j. 3

Language Focus: Synonyms (page 202)

1. joined
2. began
3. apparatus
4. ocean
5. lets (suggested answer)
6. aid or assist (suggested answer)

Second Step

Vocabulary (page 202)
tattered: torn
hospitable: friendly, welcoming
mirage: illusion or fantasy
cove: small bay of water

gloom: sadness, depression
anchor: large object used to keep a boat in one place
humidity: dampness in the air
dredging: digging the bottom of a waterway
fleet: group of boats that fish together
ramifications: results, consequences
ascendancy: rising
depleted: used up
catch limits: the highest number of fish one is allowed to catch
combed: sifted through something
timber: wood from trees
prodigal: wasteful
ideologies: philosophies

Check Your Understanding (page 206)

1. b
2. a
3. c
4. d
5. b
6. a

Language Focus: Article Practice (page 208)

1. an
2. the
3. the
4. the
5. a
6. the
7. the or nothing
8. the
9. a
10. a
11. nothing
12. The
13. an or the
14. The or A
15. a
16. the

Third Step

Vocabulary (page 209)

pesticide: poison used to kill insects
inanimate: not living
residue: leftover substance
contamination: infection or pollution
burrow: to dig
prodigious: extraordinary
insecticidal: related to pesticide
prewar: period before the war
rotenone: a type of pesticide
leguminous: related to legumes, or vegetables
sinister: evil
oxidation: the process of mixing with oxygen
malignancy: a cancerous growth
teem: to swarm, crowd
validity: power and legitimacy
biodiversity: different types of biological species
synergistic: working together to increase an effect
bioaccumulative: amassing in a biological system
herbicide: a poison used to kill plants
endocrine: type of glands
zoologist: a professional whose specialty is science related to animals
deployment: the act of putting things to use

Check Your Understanding (page 215)

The following sentences should be checked: 1, 3, 6, 8, 14, 15

Language Focus: Preposition Practice (page 216)

1. to
2. from or in
3. in
4. in
5. from
6. in
7. about
8. In
9. by
10. on
11. with
12. about
13. at or with
14. in
15. at